HERBERT FROMM
ON JEWISH MUSIC

HERBERT FROMM

ON JEWISH MUSIC

A Composer's View

TABLE OF CONTENTS

The following pieces are reprinted from the author's book SEVEN POCKETS, by permission of Dorrance & Co, Philadelphia: *The Tetragrammaton in Music, The Parable of the Shoes, Mendelssohn* (Two Letters), *Mahler* (Das Lied von der Erde).

INTRODUCTION

by
ALBERT WEISSER
Musicologist

Of Herbert Fromm's writings on Jewish music one is immediately impressed with the happy union of stylistic elegance, forceful conviction and cogent analysis. This should, of course, come as no surprise for he has long made himself known as a gifted writer of poetry, fiction, travel journals, essays and parables, with a voice of rare subtlety and imagination. In the present collected essays he has brought to his task a characteristic all-too-frequently missing in Jewish musical criticism and belle-lettres—an eminent fairness and lack of rancor; so that even when on occasion one is brought up short with a particular disagreement as to judgment or point of reference, the reader soon senses that Dr. Fromm has thought through deeply what he has written and has grappled mightily with numerous problems in Jewish music. In the end, therefore, we learn to admire his steadfastness and honesty.

Of course, Dr. Fromm has a considerable advantage over other writers on Jewish music. As a distinguished composer deeply committed to Jewish music and a sensitive and frequent executant of its literature we can be sure that he knows whereof he speaks, and whose opinion must be closely regarded. His is the insider's view of Jewish music.

The reader must be also grateful for Dr. Fromm's wide range of interest in Jewish music, from Salomon de Rossi, of whom he writes with such sympathy and fine intuition, to a variety of figures in the contemporary American synagogue. Of special interest are his writings and observations of the liturgical music of Central European Jewry and its subsequent transplantation to America, Jewish hymnology, the organ in

Jewish worship and those Jewish composers, like himself, who came to America in their youth or middle-life and proceeded to write some of their finest works or whose art underwent a new development—Ernest Bloch, Lazare Saminsky, Hugo Chaim Adler, Heinrich Schalit, among others.

Of great strength is Dr. Fromm's eloquence in expressing his hopes for the future and elevation of synagogue music. It is sure to inspire the many readers I am certain this volume will have.

PREFACE

This book is neither the work of a historian, nor a musicologist's labor. As a composer of Jewish music and its long-time practitioner as music director and organist in the service of the Synagogue, I have had many occasions to write and speak on the subject.

For this book I selected pieces that, in many instances, might be of interest not only to the musician but also to the general reader. At certain points musical examples had to be inserted to illustrate an essay in a tangible way. In most cases I restricted myself to the first page of a piece—enough to show style and direction of a composition.

No attempt was made to update my essays which cover a span of several decades. What is updated today will be obsolete tomorrow. I thought it better to leave the material in its historical setting. For the sake of orientation I gave, wherever possible, the date of writing.

The two essays in the Appendix about Mendelssohn and Mahler call for an explanation. They do not deal with Jewish music as such but with two composers of Jewish extraction. The Jew's ability to merge with the culture of his environment is shown here in two outstanding examples, almost one hundred years apart. More about this phenomenon later in the book where I discuss Mendelssohn's Jewishness.

My writings on Jewish music are by no means comprehensive. Whoever wants more complete information should turn to the works of Idelsohn, Gradenwitz, Rothmueller, Werner, Sendrey, Weisser, Holde, and others who were motivated by historical research.

What I have to offer is a composer's point of view,

which, by necessity, will be colored by the trend of his own work. This bias—if it is a fault—may be atoned for by a vivid, imaginative approach to the topic. Such, at least, is my hope.

H.F.

PART I.

WHAT IS JEWISH MUSIC?*

The question "What is Jewish music?" has been asked time and time again. It is one of those questions that is easy to ask and hard to answer. I am not trying to attain the impossible, namely a tightly knotted definition, but prefer to deal with the subject, not as a problem, but as a living experience.

Our sacred music goes back to the days of the Temple in Jerusalem, but we have no record of its actual practice. The cantillation of the Bible may well be a remnant come down to us by oral tradition. After the dispersion of the Jewish people their sacred music was exposed to the ever changing influence of other nations.

The proposition that Jewish music, for the sake of purity, should offer nothing but unharmonized chants may be the dream of academic theorists. If we want to face up to musical realities we must recognize the effects of a long Jewish history within the Western world. The extent of interpenetration between the Jewish heritage and the achievements of Western music is what interests us here.

The music of Salomone Rossi in Italy at the turn of the 16th century gives us a splendid example of Italian Renaissance music with Hebrew texts. In the 19th century there were Sulzer in Austria, Lewandowski in Germany, Naumbourg in Paris, Gerovitch in Russia—all deeply influenced by the music of their respective countries. While the unaccompanied cantorial recitative remained more true to its Oriental origin, the choral music was unmistakably colored by European ideals.

In the 20th century we have witnessed a new upsurge of

*Published in *The Cantor's Voice*, December 1963

3

Synagogue music, often sparked by the work of Avraham Zvi
Idelsohn, whose collection of Oriental Jewish melody gave a
fresh impulse to the creativity of Jewish composers in Europe
and America. It came at a time when some Jewish composers already had begun to devote their attention to the heritage
of their own Ashkenazic tradition.

There seems to be an affinity between Jewish melody and
stylistic trends of contemporary music. We believe that the ab-
sorption of authentic Ashkenazic modes and Oriental patterns,
a more meticulous regard for Hebrew declamation, and the
free use of contemporary harmonic devices, have made our
Synagogue music more distinct in a Jewish sense than the
work of the 19th century composers.

It would be easy to trace the Italian madrigal in Rossi,
German post-classicism in Lewandowski and the aftermath of
Wagner in Bloch. Yet we recognize the music of these men as
Jewish. It is not only music written by Jews with Jewish
intent—a loose definition which sometimes must suffice for
our approval—but we hear Jewish accents which suddenly
break through an otherwise eclectic style. This is less true of
Rossi but surely applies to the music of Ernest Bloch.

In the case of Jewish folk music we have a similar situation. The texts are identifiably of Jewish content. In Yiddish
folksong it is the tears and laughter of ghetto life, in Israeli
folksong the determination of the *Chalutsim* or the simple joys
of a newly discovered pastoral life. The music of Yiddish
folksong abounds in Slavic and, more particularly, Russian
elements. Israeli folksong is a fascinating compound of the
many nationalities that have come to Israel and are still in the
process of amalgamation. It is quite possible that after years of
development, Israel will some day reach a national musical
style. Whether or not this will happen is impossible to foretell.
It depends on a favorable confluence of cultural, political and
economic conditions.

The question may well be raised if it is desirable at all to
foster national trends in music, if it would not be better to
strive for a supra-national style, not distinguished by racial or
national traits. It is a question with many implications,
foremost among them a political philosophy which need not
be discussed in the context of this essay. Be it enough to re-

member that the movement for a national music in Russia, in the second half of the 19th century, brought forth Moussorgski, a composer who was deeply rooted in the folklore of his native country, but expressed himself with such force that his message transcended national boundaries and became the possession of the world. Something precious would be missing among our musical treasures if we had no Moussorgski of Russia, no Smetana of Bohemia, or Bizet of France. The Jewish voice has been heard most notably through the music of Ernest Bloch. It is a beginning and it remains for us to go on, to make our music so strong that it will become a distinct voice in the consort of nations, an accepted part of the music of the world.

Jewish music today is a mixture of many ingredients, and thus a true mirror of Jewish history. The quest for absolute originality is a sport indulged in by less informed critics. This kind of originality does not exist. All art emerges from a maze of complicated relationships, and if a work miraculously seems to float in air by its own power, it is only that we do not see the fine strings that hold it there.

What, then, shall we look for in Jewish music? It may come down to as much or as little as a certain inflection, a particular turn of phrase, or even in a negative way, the avoidance of certain chords or cadences, all of which, to the attuned ear, mark music as Jewish. This becomes more subtle in instrumental music where the absence of a text robs the listener of the more obvious connections.

There is no infallible yardstick of stylistic criteria by which to measure Jewish music. It is a matter of spirit responding to spirit, or—if you will—the unconscious recognition of origins which shun the light of analytic search.

INTRODUCTION TO ADATH ISRAEL*

A Friday Eve Service

Before going into an analysis of the music, I would like to dwell on certain general ideas which guided me in the composition of the work.

After its publication I heard quite a few comments by Jewish musicians. Some welcomed the Jewishness of the work, some thought it should be more Jewish, others again found it too Jewish.

I, myself, am aware of two facts:

1) As music director and organist of a Jewish Temple I am in constant practical touch with the music for the Synagogue and its requirements.
2) As a composer I want to contribute creatively to the cultural wealth of our people.

How much Jewishness there is in my music is not for me to say. The answer to this question may be found in that layer of the mind over which I have no conscious power. But let us not spend too much time on these hidden things. A tree wants to grow and will not stop every now and then to dig up the soil, making sure that the roots which feed it are really its own.

As I said in my preface, I approached the task as a modern Jew. That our traditional modes would have to play an important part was self-evident but there was room enough for an independent treatment of the material. The *Ahava*

*A lecture given by the composer in 1943 at the Jewish Music Forum of New York City.

7

rabba mode was eliminated in spite of its traditional associations. Its morose character has always appeared to me—and not only to me—as incompatible with the healthy sturdiness of our prayers and psalms. Its musical possibilities are too limited to offer much inducement, and the stagnancy of many a piece of Jewish music is due to the predominance of that mode.

Recitatives in the traditional style are surely to be found in my work, trimmed, however, of an excessive use of florid figuration which so often stops the flow and meaning of the words. It was my wish to embody traditional material within the framework of a free creation.

We have only to compare Sulzer with Schubert, Lewandowski with Brahms, Schorr with Moussorgski to see at once that these Jewish composers were behind their time. In their hands harmony remained a square block which they could not melt into a language, capable of expressing the more delicate turns of thought and emotion. I am not saying this with disdain but with full understanding that Jewish music, which for such a long time was unison-music, had to wait its turn for the development of harmony.

In our time, harmony with all its intricacies is no longer an unknown treasure for the Jewish composer and we find subtle and truly contemporary progressions in many a new creation. Let future historians decide if we succeeded in creating an adequate musical expression for the Jewish life of our time. Whatever their verdict, our honest search should earn their respect.

I am naturally conscious of the difference between music for the concert hall and music for Synagogue and Church but there is no doubt that religious music in its loftiest utterances (Bach, Mozart, Bruckner) does not have to shun the bright light of the concert stage. Its spiritual quality is such that it will radiate its message under any circumstances. We must be frank to admit that there is little in Jewish music today that will stand up under such a test.

I made a special effort to unify my work in a symphonic sense by letting certain basic motifs carry the musical structure. We all know the checkered and distracting impression that results from a service made up of ten pieces by ten different composers in ten different styles.

The prayer book is a unity that offers religious thoughts in a logical and well-ordered sequence. The music should follow in a similar way. My work is not a loose collection of pieces strung together under one cover, but rather a cycle in many movements whose individual numbers are tied together by musical means.

Unity is one of our social and political dreams. Achieving it in the outer world with all its obstacles of ill-will and malice will perhaps remain an eternal problem. But in the sphere of music, which hovers lightly over this heavy planet of ours, we should be allowed to glimpse at times the faint outline of that unity which we all seek.

If my work could be considered an attempt in that direction I shall feel amply rewarded.

(Here followed a detailed musical analysis of the work which is not within the scope of this book).

THE ROLE OF THE CREATIVE MUSICIAN IN THE SYNAGOGUE*

When speaking of the creative musician in the Synagogue, I wish to employ the term "creative" in its higher sense, devoid of its connotation in daily advertising. What I have in mind is a composer bold enough to call David his ancestor and Asaph, chief musician under David and Solomon, his professional forebear. It is a proud concept indeed; a composer under its spell will not be satisfied with musical mediocrity in a house of worship, and will never cease to chafe under the inevitable restrictions imposed on his ideal.

It might be helpful if we divide our composer's work into four categories:

Music for use at weekly Services and Holidays

Organ Music

Complete musical settings of the liturgy in larger forms

Free creation of sacred, not necessarily liturgical, texts.

Concerning the first category, I am thinking of pieces properly fitted in length to the overall structure of the Service. Mature discipline is required to say in concise musical terms what the text demands. When writing for liturgical use the composer must learn to direct his talent into prescribed channels. The difficult and elusive balance between beauty and usefulness should be achieved. It is a constant search for which no ready

*This lecture was given on November 16, 1965 at the Biennial Convention of the Union of American Hebrew Congregations in San Francisco. It was published in the American Guild of Organists' Quarterly in April 1966.

11

formula exists. But the hand of a true composer will always show, even in the smallest response.

It is too easy to imitate the style of the 19th century, dressed up, perhaps, with a few fancier chords. We have enough composers who avoid the steep road. Our task must be to strive for an acceptable, not merely experimental, contemporary idiom, to arrive at a style that will not be obsolete after a few years of trial and error.

Our first category also embraces the field of Hymnology. The present Union Hymnal is a compendium of stylistic confusion. Most of its material consists of leftovers from the Protestant Church. But there are some promising seeds which may come to fruition in a new hymnal. It will not be enough to approach the task negatively by avoiding the four-part Lutheran hymn. We must begin to set up affirmative standards of our own. Here is a territory offering unexpected satisfaction to a creative musician. It is harder than it looks to write a strong and characteristically Jewish hymn. If a composer succeeds in creating a hymn destined to resound in all Synagogues he may have achieved a modest kind of immortality—even if he did no more than enter the House of Fame by way of the kitchen door.

It must be observed that all music coming under the heading of our first category has its best representatives among those composers who are actively engaged in serving the music departments of our Synagogues. They know the liturgy, its requirements, and have developed a feeling for what one might call "the liturgical tone." I would be hard put to explain just what I mean by "liturgical tone," but it does exist, and it is a demonstrable fact that outsiders who write an occasional piece for the liturgy hardly ever hit the mark.

As a second category of the Synagogue composer's work, we listed organ music. It is customary for the organists of most Temples to play organ music for about 15 minutes before the Service and to end the Service with a postlude. Our organists use for the most part the rich organ literature of the Church although a new literature of indigenous Jewish organ music is beginning to develop. Organ music based on Jewish themes or, in a wider sense, written in a Jewish idiom is needed and our composers should give more serious attention to this neglected aspect of our music.

In the third category—complete musical settings of the liturgy in larger forms—I do not refer to collections of individual pieces which happen to have a rendezvous under one book cover but otherwise are not related stylistically. A valid work of this kind should be conceived symphonically whereby each detail must be a necessary link for the building of a cohesive structure.

The composer should not worry too much about he difficulty of performance but write as he must by calling on all his musical resources. As it turns out, there will always be a few single pieces which can be taken out of context and are accessible for modest forces. But the aim of a symphonic Service must be a complete performance, be it with organ or with orchestra, prepared by a sufficient number of rehearsals and presented at a special occasion.

The fourth category—free creations on sacred, not necessarily liturgical, texts—concerns itself with cantatas and the like. Texts ranging from the Bible through medieval writings to contemporary literature may be found in profusion. From my personal point of view I must say that the new translations of the Bible in their dry, sober language do not offer much incentive for musical settings. It is not within my province to discuss the scholarly merits of the new translations but they cannot replace the strength and imaginative latitude of the older versions.

In dealing with the third and fourth categories, I cannot emphasize enough that composers must resist being dragged down by utilitarian demands. Complexity of texture need not be avoided. A Mass by Palestrina, a Motet by Bach may serve as classical examples of sacred music executed with uncompromising musical integrity. A composer is not a handyman and must not allow himself to be deterred by the criticism of those who have no ear for music of this kind.

It is a sad fact that sacred music—be it of Christian or Jewish origin—is considered second rate or worse by musicians in the secular field. By way of illustration I offer a small, yet illuminating incident: Some time ago I met a composer of my acquaintance in the street. Upon his question what I have been writing I told him that I had just finished a Sabbath Service commissioned by a Temple out of town. Thinking that I had not properly understood his question, he persisted: "No, no, I mean what *music* have you written of late?"

It is a painful thing for me to concede that such unflattering opinions have a basis in the bulk of sacred music that does not measure up to high standards of contemporary excellence. We have a few works to counter the argument but many more are needed before we can point to a literature of sufficient breadth and weight.

If our Synagogues offer the kind of freedom outlined here we may conceivably attract young gifted composers who in some cases may even be endowed with enough religious loyalties to choose a career in the dimly lit corners of the nation's musical life. But I must also speak of the rewards a composer may expect when working for the Synagogue: He is not creating in a vacuum but writing for an immediate purpose, which is more than many contemporary composers can claim. The anonymity a composer is sure to find when working for Church or Synagogue may be a healthy antidote to the American craze for publicity which tries to make us believe that a man's importance can be measured by the frequency of his name appearing in newspapers and magazines.

I will not conceal the fact that our profession, like any other, has its portion of routine and drudgery. But if we are dedicated to the service of God we will learn to understand that a coin retains its value even if the picture of the reigning royalty has been flattened out by constant use.

DO WE HAVE A JEWISH MUSIC CULTURE IN AMERICA?*

My theme "Do We have a Jewish Music Culture in America?" is restricted on two counts:

1) It refers only to the *musical* culture of the Jews
2) In a particular place, the United States of America

Leaving Jewish music aside for the moment, let us first look at the general musical scene in America today. We have a large and busy musical life; the music section of the *New York Times* on Sunday during the concert season is convincing proof of the many-branched channels of our musical civilization. However, we must consider that this buzzing musical life of ours has brought music down to the status of a commodity, easily to be had in any quantity or quality in the concert hall or at home by means of radio, record player and television.

This commodity, music, is promoted by a host of publishers, managers and stars of all sizes in the performing field. The names of some performing artists are "nationally advertised" (as the phrase goes in commercial life) and almost as well known as certain breakfast cereals.

The main emphasis for audience and critic alike is on the *performance* of music. The creator, dead or alive, is of secondary importance, his message in music of lesser interest than the technicalities of performance. In our musical civilization the natural order of things has been upset; we have turned an obelisk around and are trying to balance it on the sharp needle point of performing skill while the broad base of

*This essay was written around 1950.

15

creativity sways precariously high up in the air.

But it would be unjust to say that this musical life, brightly illuminated by the neon signs of publicity, is all we have. We do have a modest musical culture, not widely publicized, which—in a manner of speaking—subsists by the light of kerosene lamps. Universities, colleges, music schools are pursuing cultural aims with idealism and dedication. Old music, rarely heard, and new contemporary works are being performed with equal zeal. The performances—adequate, good, rarely brilliant—lay stress on music as music.

I do not mean to say that brilliant performance and musical culture are mutually exclusive. But I do believe that an unwavering insistence on nothing but brilliant performance, so characteristic of our musical life, springs from a lack of essential musical understanding.

Coming back to Jewish Music, we must raise the question: Can we resist the leveling influence of our civilization? I draw a dividing line between the busy civilization of our official music life and the more quiet culture of less official music making. These two concepts can, of course, be applied to Jewish music as well. We have the Synagogue, an institution which stands aside from the noise of musical business enterprise and could well act as an independent sponsor of the arts. Before going further, let us first ask specifically: What are the conditions for the flourishing of musical culture? Looking at past centuries we may define the components of musical culture as follows:

1) A steady stream of free creativity
2) A natural demand for the composer's output.

In the last few decades an enormous amount of music has been given to the American Synagogue in a continuous flow of new works, some of them significant, original and of high artistic calibre. Composers of substance and skill are putting their talents into the development of a new liturgical style. A Synagogue music is emerging which successfully blends ancient materials with the devices of modern music. I earnestly believe that the history of synagogue music could at no time boast of such an era of ever growing enrichment as in our own days. This, then, fulfills the main condition of a living culture: the creative fountainhead exists and is not yet exhausted by any means.

How about our second point: a natural demand for the composer's output? Here we find ourselves in serious difficulties. The average congregant resists the introduction of new music and prefers to hear the "old traditional music"— whatever that term may mean to him. He is not aware of new stirrings which must find a musical counterpart in liturgical creations by contemporary composers. Only a slow process of education can help this situation.

Another obstacle to the acceptance of new music into the repertoire of the Synagogue is the scarcity of high-minded cantors, organists, and choir directors who feel their responsibility on this outpost of Jewish culture. One rarely hears of a young talented Jewish musician who chooses the Synagogue as his field of activity. Most young musicians are possessed by the idea that only the career of the celebrated virtuoso is worth trying for; if this condition persists, the time will come when the last Jewish organist can be seen stuffed and under glass in the Jewish Museum in New York, labelled as a now extinct species of Jewish musician.

It is scarcely believable how unknown the mere existence of so many volumes of new Jewish liturgical music is even to the educated Jew who, let us assume, reads good books, the better kind of magazines and is genuinely interested in Jewish matters.

A magazine like Commentary reviews at great length all new books of more or less Jewish interest and calls on authorities in the field for competent and constructive reviews. Important publications of Jewish music are completely ignored, not only by Commentary but by other Jewish magazines as well.

It is quite possible that, while perishable best-sellers of the day are discussed in great detail, lasting values in Jewish music may go entirely unnoticed. Just because the output of contemporary Jewish music is so large it would be necessary to have the new works reviewed by experts who reject bad and inept works and isolate the important works from the ever growing bulk of Jewish music which is suffering under its own weight. Critical guidance is needed but most of all a pointing out to the lay public that here is a phenomenon of Jewish culture which for some time managed to grow in darkness but now needs the light of benevolent care.

Where, then, do we stand in matters of Jewish music culture in America today? My answer is that as long as composer and public cannot meet on a basis of mutual need we cannot yet speak of a culture. The possibilities exist because the creative musicians are doing their part; but against them stand the powers of congregational resistance or indifference, the scarcity of idealistic cantors, organists and choirmasters and finally the ignorance of the lay public.

Whether Jewish music is destined to become part of the music culture of the world, and what contribution American Jewish creativity will make towards that goal is impossible to predict. But that should not worry us too much. For the time being, we have enough work to do to make our music even stronger and to find a spacious home for it among our own people.

JEWISH HYMNOLOGY*

Its Past, Its Future

The question whether or not the singing of congregational hymns in the Synagogue is a legitimately Jewish practice does not constitute the problem I am discussing here. I am starting from the factual premise that a call for more and better congregational singing has been sounded for quite a few years within the Reform movement.

It can safely be said that the musical standards of our professional choirs have improved during the last decades. Some of our Synagogues not only carry out ambitious musical projects once or twice a year, but also have raised the musical quality of their weekly Services to a higher level.

No such development has been taking place in the field of congregational singing, although all sorts of practical suggestions have been advanced to make our congregations sing: training of a nucleus of congregants to be placed during the Service in different parts of the Temple, hymn exercises before or after the Service, leading of the congregation by the Cantor or a soloist of the choir, and the like. In spite of these attempts, we hear only in rare instances of a reasonably successful cure. All these experiments touch only the surface of the problem. We have to look deeper if we want to understand why our average congregation will not indulge in singing.

Idelsohn, without elaborating further on the statement, calls "group participation one of the principal features of

*Published in the Proceedings of the Sixth Annual Convention of the American Conference of Cantors, June 15-18, 1959.

Jewish worship since Bible times." We know that in the ancient Temple the congregation used to chant short refrains,
such as *Amen, Halleluyah, Hoshianah, Anenu* and so on. The
worshippers also sang by way of repetition or alternation
Psalm verses, first intoned by the leader.

In medieval times with the rise of the *Chazzan* the musical
part of the Service was taken over almost completely by the
Cantor; the congregation, in need of self expression, would
sing along with the solo renditions of the Cantor.

The picture changed radically with the advent of Reform
Judaism which followed in the course of the Emancipation.
An urgent demand for congregational singing as part of a
well ordered Service was voiced. The musical response to this
new need was at first—as could be expected—confused, timid
and purely imitative.

This particular period of our musical development corresponds in some ways to the time of Luther's Reformation in
the beginning of the 16th century. Up to the time of
Luther—due to the strict separation between clergy and
layman—the musical part of the congregation in worship was
limited to a few short refrains in Latin. Luther was not only
the creator of a new Church Liturgy but also the founder of
congregational hymn singing. The new material, needed in
quick order, he took from Gregorian chants, sequences, old
and contemporary folksongs. The Latin texts were translated
into German, the secular German texts transformed into sacred poetry. The task of translation, simplification, adaptation
of established melodies to new words, and above all, the creation of new church poetry and new tunes—all this was undertaken by Luther and his helpers in a storm of creative energy.
The musical success of Luther's movement was overwhelming
and far reaching; he was not only a robust and shrewd fighter
but also a highly gifted poet and musician who himself produced some of the strongest and most stirring hymns in the
literature of the Church.

When in the beginning of the 19th century the Jewish Reform movement began to spread in Germany, the adaptation
and composition of new hymns for Temple worship was, for
lack of interest on the part of Jewish composers, in many cases
entrusted to church musicians of the Christian faith. The re-

sult was the introduction of those straight-laced and rigid
hymns which soon became traditional in Reform congregations and whose ghosts have not ceased to haunt our hymnals
up to the present day.

The musical poverty of the Reform movement in its beginnings is astounding when compared with the strong impulses that led to so many important changes in worship. In
order to understand it, we must make a clear distinction between Reform and Reformation. A reformator, such as
Luther, became the maker of a political revolution that began
with spoken words and pamphlets but finally spread to the
battlefields of the Thirty Years' War. Such a folk movement
made music and hymns quite naturally spring up in its wake,
without the self-conscious and often artificial efforts that
marked the musical beginnings of our Jewish reformers.
Compared with the course of Luther's Reformation, our Reform was only something like a sectarian secession, a house-
cleaning, as it were. True, there was enough fighting and bitterness, but Judaism was not split into two, as was Christianity
when the Protestant Church established itself as a new power,
hostile to the Roman Church. Seen in this light we perceive
the reason for the musical blandness of our Jewish hymnology
which is a by-product of the Jewish Reform movement, and as
such not older than just a little more than one hundred years.

It is not our purpose here to survey the many individual
hymnals that came and went during these hundred years. The
most serious attempt to change the direction was undertaken
in this country with the appearance of the Union Hymnal in
1932. This book is a curious hybrid. The foreword states that
"the Committee was actuated by a desire to revive the value of
Jewish melody, make use of neglected Jewish poetry, lean
heavily where possible, upon Jewish Motifs and finally contribute to the field of hymnology a publication which would be
essentially Jewish in color, spirit and purpose." An excellent
program, indeed—but actually carried out with so many com-
promises and musical shortcomings that only careful search
will here and there discover some of the values which the
editors had set out to give to their Reform congregations.

Much too much of the old material that should have been
overcome with a radical sweep was still retained. Cobwebs and

more cobwebs throughout the book! The attempts at traditional Jewish material are new and certainly a step in the right direction. However, the newness of the task permitted only an experimental approach to the problem and the editors themselves say in the preface with all sincerity that their book is only "an advance on the road toward the achievement of a difficult goal."

Many of the melodies taken from the Jewish tradition are entirely unsingable for congregational requirements, also in several cases badly fitted to English words. The subjective and highly emotional elements, so attractive in our cantorial art, do not easily lend themselves to the purpose of mass singing. The harmony chosen for the pieces based on Jewish tradition or written newly in the Hebraic idiom, is either the wooden four-part writing of the church style, wholly unsuitable for Jewish melody—or, frankly experimental and arbitrary. There are, of course, laudable exceptions, such as Achron's "God Supreme" and some pieces by Heinrich Schalit—but they are intimate solo songs rather than hymns. A. W. Binder and Jacob Weinberg came forward with some good usable material.

I am fully aware of the difficulties confronting the editors of the Union Hymnal and I recognize without reservation their honest striving for something better than had been offered in preceding hymnals. But we must not stop where the Hymnal of 1932 left off. Our experiences have taught us that the Union Hymnal with its leniency toward outlived old material and its not quite matured experimentation with Jewish melody does not answer the needs of today. A new hymnal has become a necessity.

For one thing, we must get away from the attitude that we have to be just as good as the Joneses next door, that is, that our hymnal must be as bulky as any church hymnal. The Church looks back at a long tradition of 400 years, but we are newcomers in the field of hymnology and should, therefore, be content with modest beginnings. Let us remember that the first hymnal after Luther's Reformation had only 18 hymns.

It was, as I said before, a folk movement of great political import that from the time of the Reformation onward led to the adaptation and new creation of hymns for the Protestant

Church. The Jewish Reform Synagogue could at no time claim to be a religious movement of such vehement political impact as was the Lutheran challenge to the Roman Church. Only in our days have we witnessed in Zionism a strongly idealistic as well as political Jewish movement that spontaneously brought forth song after song. Here, then, is a source that must be made available for congregational singing in the Synagogue. In the same way as Luther adapted secular songs to sacred words, can we adapt some of the Israeli melodies to English words that will fit into the framework of a sacred Service. From this point of view I adapted "Naaleh L'Artsenu"–a song of the early *Chalutsim*–to English words paraphrasing the 92nd Psalm. This is a new hymn to which the congregation of Temple Israel, Boston, otherwise not noted for lusty singing, responds with a good measure of zest and vigor.

(Example No. 1)

I admit that not many Israeli melodies are as good and sturdy as *Naaleh L'Artsenu*, but I am convinced that more material can be reshaped and made available with good results. This will not say that the new hymnal I envision should exclusively lean on Israeli sources: but I do maintain that it would be a sin of omission to ignore such a forceful stream of Jewish life.

An important part of the small new hymnal would, of course, be given over to already established, traditional hymns for Festivals and Sabbaths, such as *Maoz Tsur, Addir Hu, Yigdal, Adon Olam, En Kelohenu, Shalom Aleychem* and so on. Some of them, for instance, *Addir Hu, En Kelohenu, Shalom Aleychem* are of inferior musical quality. If they cannot be rooted out they should, at least, be presented in new, and less trivial musical arrangements. We also ought to consider other and better optional tunes to be printed next to these accepted melodies, so that a choice for the better is possible.

The Yigdal tune, known as "Leoni", has become a favorite of the Church, but is sadly neglected in the Synagogue, the place of its origin. We should win it back—not in its church-gowned four-part harmony but in a more idiomatic harmonic setting and cleansed melodically.

(Example No. 2)

Furthermore, *Zemiroth* melodies should find a place in our hymnal. They are the sacred folk melodies of our tradition and have a claim to be heard in our Temples as well as in our homes.

(Example No. 3)

And lastly—*Shiru Ladonai Shir Chadash!* New hymns should be commissioned from contemporary Jewish composers and judged by a competennt board of editors. The Union Hymnal was the first to venture out into this field. Some fine and valuable compositions resulted, but rarely fitted for the particular purpose of congregational singing. Most of the new contributors were hiding behind the safe walls of the widely approved Church hymn style. It is a difficult task for any modern composer to create a convincing new hymn. Of many attempts, very few will succeed. But even these few would mean a great addition to a Jewish hymnology that, admittedly, is still in its infancy.

Summing up, then, these are the main points of a program for a new hymnal:

1. Already established traditional hymns in better musical arrangements—away from the conventional Church chorale style.
2. *Zemiroth*, in English adaptations, or in their original Hebrew.
3. Israeli melodies in English adaptations to sacred words.
4. New hymns to be commissioned from contemporary Jewish composers.

I firmly believe that such a hymnal would be a greater incentive to congregational singing than all the patchwork of practical devices laboring over old and borrowed material which has outlived its usefulness. It should be a challenge for the Jewish musicians of today to make a new, cooperative effort. Past experiences and new insights will probably lead to more acceptable results.

1. PRAISE YE THE LORD

(PSALM 92)

PENINA MOISE

ISRAELI MELODY
Arr. by Herbert Fromm

Allegro maestoso

Praise ye the Lord, for__ it is good His might - y
Break forth, O Is - ra - el in - to song, let hymns as-

acts to mag - ni - fy, and make those mer - cies__
cend to heav - en's vault; no sweet - er task has__

un - der - stood, His hand de - lights to mul - ti - ply.
mor - tal tongue than its Cre - a - tor to ex - alt.

Praise_ ye the Lord,   praise_ ye the Lord,
Praise_ ye the Lord,   praise_ ye the Lord,

praise_ ye the Lord,   praise_ ye the Lord!
praise_ ye the Lord,   praise_ ye the Lord!

Praise ye the Lord, for__ it is good
Praise ye the Lord, for__ it is good

His might-y acts to mag - ni - fy.
His might-y acts to mag - ni - fy.

2. Praise To The Living God

Translated from the Hebrew
by NEWTON MANN

(YIGDAL)

TRADITIONAL MELODY
arr. by Herbert Fromm

Herbert Fromm

3. Sweet Hymns and Songs

(ANIM Z'MIROTH)

Translated from the Hebrew by
ALICE LUCAS

TRADITIONAL MELODY
arr. by Herbert Fromm

Moderato

Sweet hymns and songs will I__ re - cite to
O may my words of bless - ing__ rise to
My me - di - ta - tion day__ and__ night, may

sing of__ Thee by day__ and__ night, of Thee who art my__
Thee, who__ throned a - bove__ the__ skies, art just and might-y,__
it__ be__ pleas - ant in__ Thy__ sight, for Thou art all my__

soul's_ de - light, of Thee_ who__ art my soul's_ de - light.
great_ and_ wise, art just_ and_ might - y, great_ and_ wise.
soul's_ de - light, for Thou_ art_ all my soul's_ de - light.

CONTEMPORARY SYNAGOGUE MUSIC IN AMERICA*

(With a Short Historical Survey)

The history of Hebrew sacred music dates from the time of King David, some 3000 years ago. Biblical sources tell us of a splendid musical pageant performed by a multitude of singers and instrumentalists, and we need only turn to the 150th Psalm to find within a few lines of poetry a flash of those early rites transmitted through the haze of centuries.

It was under the reigns of King David and of Solomon that Hebrew music flowered fully. David, the poet-musician, raised music to such significance that religion and music became inseparable. David has indeed become the symbolic figure of the Sacred Poet and Musician, and a Greek Church Father, St. John, Bishop of Constantinople, voiced the general opinion when writing about 400 A.D.:

> "When the faithful are keeping vigil in the Church,
> David is first, middle and last—
> At funeral processions and burials, David is first, middle and last—
> In the holy monasteries, among the ranks of the heavenly warriors, David is first, middle and last."

After the destruction of the Second Temple in the year 70 A.D. the remnants of the Jewish people were scattered all over the Roman Empire. The musical tradition was preserved from mouth to mouth but the rabbis forbade instrumental

*This essay was published in the *Journal of Synagogue Music*, November 1969.

music for worship as a sign of mourning for the loss of the sanctuary in Jerusalem. Hebrew music was reduced to unaccompanied singing.

With the development of worship as a daily ritual there arose the need for a man who would stand before the congregation, recite the prayers and chant the Bible. This office, in contrast to the Temple in Jerusalem, where only the priests and Levites took an active part in the Service, was occupied by a layman chosen by the congregation and called *Sh'liach Tsibbur*, the messenger of the congregation. As music and prayers grew more complex, the need for a professional precentor was felt and thus, in the early middle ages, the office of the *Chazzan*, or Cantor, came into being. Most of the cantors from the 10th to the 14th centuries were poets, singers and composers. The cultivation of so many talents make the medieval cantors counterparts to the French Troubadours and the German Minnesingers, with the exception that the cantor could use his talents only for the sanctity of worship.

The music so far dealt with was strictly melodic and without any harmonic accompaniment. The first known attempt on a broad basis to introduce harmony into the music of the Synagogue was made in Italy by Salamone Rossi in the beginning of the 17th century. Rossi, court musician in Mantua and a composer of secular fame, aimed at a reform of Jewish liturgical music by adding "the rules of musical art." Although protected by the famous and versatile Rabbi Leone de Modena who wrote a preface to Rossi's work (1622) the reform did not spread.

Rossi's approach was completely European and certainly a great exception in his time. Most Jews continuing in the belief that their stay in exile was only temporary and that they would finally return to Zion, preserved the Oriental elements in their music although yielding at times to influences of the Western world. The French Revolution and the Emancipation, however, changed the outlook among less orthodox Jews and led to radical innovations in worship.

The Reform Movement starting in the first half of the 19th century set itself apart from the Orthodox Synagogue with the idea of remodeling Judaism according to modern needs. As far as music is concerned, an enrichment of means was the consequence; organ and mixed choir were introduced. While the unaccompanied cantorial solos still preserved the ancient modes with their special flavor and leaning towards florid improvisation, the music for choir and organ was pressed into the mold of Western art. The free flow of the Hebrew language was hindered by 19th century conventions. Musical forms built on regular periods of even numbered measures proved to be a rigid frame for the irregular meters of Hebrew texts.

Two monumental works are the outstanding examples of this period. *Shir Zion* (Song of Zion) by Salomon Sulzer and *Todah v'zimrah* (Praise and Song) by Louis Lewandowski. Both men were deeply influenced by the German music of the 19th century. Their choral music is clean, concise, dignified—but not always characteristic.

In the beginning of its harmonic ventures Synagogue music walked on stilts. It was so with Rossi in the 17th century, with Sulzer, Lewandowski and a host of other composers in the 19th century. In our own time new efforts have been made to arrive at a more idiomatic liturgical style, and we have witnessed a profound renewal of Synagogue music in America, roughly beginning around the year 1930.

This statement prompts me to a word of caution concerning our situation which has been labeled a Renaissance of Jewish Music. Certainly, there are factors that speak for our conviction that such a renaissance has actually taken place. But I can imagine another writer, fifty years hence, pointing out where we have erred and gone astray. He may find a few drafty corners in our house but I believe that the progress made since the turn of the century will be acknowledged as a step toward a purer and more typical music for Jewish worship.

The contemporary trend may be summarized in this fashion:

1. Return to the proper modes of the Ashkenazic tradition.
2. Utilization of the chants of Oriental communities made available through the volumes of A. Z. Idelsohn.
3. Application of harmonic and contrapuntal devices

suitable for melodic material originally conceived
without accompaniment.
4. Free invention of melodies in the spirit of authentic
   sources.
5. Greater care in the understanding of Hebrew inflection and syntax.
6. Creation of professional music departments in our
   Synagogues capable of meeting the demands of
   this music.

Coming now to the evaluation of contemporary composers who have contributed to our cause I must apologize to
those who cannot be mentioned within the scope of this essay.
Unpublished music, not being generally accessible, must be
eliminated.

The process of purification of Synagogue music owes a
debt to *Lazare Saminsky* who had distinct ideas about Jewish
melos, as laid down in his controversial book *Music of the
Ghetto and the Bible.* His Synagogue music, written in an au-
stere diatonic style, shows simplicity, starkness, brevity of form
and regard for liturgical usefulness. Nothing green seems to
grow in Saminsky's music but we honor in it a striving toward
a clearly envisioned ideal of sacred expression, a dissatisfaction
with the borrowed comforts of the 19th century. As proof we
offer the first page of his 92nd Psalm.

(Example No. 1)

Joseph Achron in his Friday Eve Service excels by melodic
invention of a definitely Jewish flavor. His harmony, however,
fails to enhance the freshness of his melodic material. There
is a groping for the right chords but he rarely finds a truly
convincing solution.

Achron's dilemma between voice and accompaniment
brings to mind a remark by Max Helfman. Referring to
Genesis 27:22, where Isaac blesses Jacob who had come in the
guise of Esau, Helfman quoted:

> The voice is the voice of Jacob
> but the hands are the hands of Esau.

However, in a hymn of no more than ten measures, set to
the words "God supreme, to Thee we pray" (Union Hymnal

No. 93) Achron succeeded in shaping on a miniature scale a piece of rare perfection. It is an intimate composition, not particularly useful as a congregational hymn, but unforgettable as a devout sacred solo.

Jacob Weinberg, influenced by the theories of Joseph Yasser, offered in his Friday Eve Service his best work for the Synagogue. Loosely based on the pentatonic scale, the music is richly textured and spread out in expansive forms. His Sabbath Morning Service which followed much later was conceived on an even larger scale but lacks the communication of the earlier work.

A. W. Binder became a major influence on the rejuvenation of Synagogue music in America. He propagated in musical works as well as in his teaching the return to the best sources of Jewish tradition. His works are imbued with motifs from both prayer modes and biblical cantillation, with an occasional leaning on Israeli folk music. His musical services show a steady upward curve in terms of personal achievement within the general framework of contemporary trends.

The work of *Heinrich Schalit* occupies a special place. His music, whether based on tradition or freely invented, bears the stamp of an always recognizable personal style. Rooted in a romanticism which has no relationship to Wagner's overheated, chromatic sensuality, Schalit's work shines with the radiance of devotion to religious ideals.

The musical illustration taken from his Friday Evening Liturgy is the opening of *L'cha dodi*, using Idelsohn's notation of an Oriental-Sephardic chant. It shows the composer's original mind in its fresh diatonic harmony and a rhythmic finesse resulting from the canonic treatment of a model which spans no more than the interval of the diminished fifth.

(Example No. 2)

We have two Sabbath Eve Services by *Frederick Jacobi*, the first an *a capella* work, the second with organ accompaniment. The earlier work offers much musical interest although the effort to find a Jewish idiom sometimes deteriorates into artificial devices, such as syncopations of more Scottish than Jewish provenance, cold, unfelt coloraturas, etc. The later work written shortly before the composer's death, aims at a forced homophonic simplicity. The harmonic staleness and constant repetition of phrases indicate a fatigue of creative powers. Jacobi's Hebrew anthem *Teyfen l'hakshiv*(Turn to listen), set to a poem by Saadia Gaon (882-942), may well be his best work for the Synagogue.

Lazar Weiner, the undisputed master of the secular Yiddish art song, is going different ways in his liturgical works which, in a larger context, may be seen as a continuation of what Achron had begun. Weiner's melody has the authentic ring of Jewish declamation and he is steadily searching for musical textures best fitted to his material. In his later works he has arrived at a freely dissonant and often elaborate harmonic scheme.

Gershon Ephros, pupil of Idelsohn, professional cantor and compiler of the indispensable, many-volumed *Cantorial Anthology*, is a composer who has so far published two large-scale works for the Synagogue, *S'lichot* (Midnight Pentitential Service) and *L'yom hashabbat*, a Sabbath Morning Service for use in the conservative Synagogue. A Friday Evening Service, at the time of this writing, is awaiting publication. Similar to the method of Ernest Bloch, whole sections of the liturgy are bound together in large movements whose individual pieces are connected by interludes. These interludes give the impression of afterthoughts and do not always come off successfully. Ephros is one of the best representatives of those composers who nurture *Nussach hatefillah*, the traditional prayer modes. His works, however, suffer from an almost constant density of polyphonic writing.

Isadore Freed added a special note to the music of the Synagogue, a natural grace and elegance which perhaps had not been heard since the time of Salamone Rossi. Having studied in France, Freed applied a subtle overlay of French harmony to Jewish material although he remained deeply concerned with traditional modes as shown in his valuable treatise on the subject. Aside from vocal music for the Synagogue he also contributed a set of "Six Liturgical Organ Pieces" belonging to the most useful efforts in a small but growing literature.

Max Helfman, an uneven composer, had his roots in the Polish-Russian tradition with its unrestrained emotional appeal and flair for theatrical effects. His work *Aron hakodesh* (The Holy Ark) accompanying the ceremony of the scriptural reading exemplifies these traits most strikingly. Some pages of *L'cha Adonai* are among the best things Helfman ever wrote.

Hugo Chaim Adler was a cantor of distinctively creative gifts. His hallmark is a moderately contemporary polyphony set to melodic material of the Southern German tradition.

Julius Chajes, best known for his secular Jewish music, has not given much to the Synagogue, but his one slim volume has the merit of a clearly defined style. It is a stubborn diatonicism delivered with the conviction of a firmly rooted musical philosophy.

Herman Berlinski's Sabbath Eve Service is the work of a composer wholeheartedly committed to the shaping of a Jewish melos. It is an ambitious work carried out with excellent workmanship. I personally prefer a less overburdened, more lucid way of writing but I sincerely respect Berlinski's achievement.

Reuven Kosakoff's Lichvod Shabbat (In Honor of Sabbath) shows the composer in an emphatic attempt to reconcile old and new ways. There are occasional incongruities, such as *Mi chamocha* in the 19th century manner following an experimental organ interlude for *Kriat Sh'ma*. But there are successful solutions, such as the antiphonal 98th Psalm, an imaginative Chaconne built as a solid structure for *Hashkivenu*, a sensitive *Kaddish* and the variations on a good *Adon Olam* tune.

Having dealt so far with works of practical dimensions, we must now speak about the sprawling Sabbath Morning Services of *Ernest Bloch* and *Darius Milhaud*. Bloch's Service, written for chorus, baritone cantor and large orchestra oversteps by far the limits set by the ordinary demands of the liturgy—which is not a fault in the case of so precious a gift. Bloch approaches the text in the fervent and personal way of a man deeply stirred by his Jewsih experience and the symbolism of an ancient faith. It is "the harsh and haughty accents of the Hebrew tongue" we hear in Bloch's music. Bloch is not a seeker after the color and perfumery of the exotic. His Hebraicism, far from being an acquisition from without, is the upsurge of an ancestral Hebraic severity, of Biblical grief and exultation.

In Bloch's own words: "I do not propose or desire to attempt a reconstruction of the music of the Jews and to base my works on melodies more or less authentic. It is the Hebrew spirit that interests me, the complex and agitated soul that vibrates in the Bible; the vigor and ingenuousness of the Patriarchs, the desperation of the preachers of Jerusalem, the sorrow and grandeur of the book of Job, the sensuality of the Song of Songs. All this is in us, all this is in me and is the better part of me. Does anyone think he is only himself? Far from it! He is thousands of his ancestors. If he writes as he feels, no matter how exceptional his point of view, his expression will be basically that of his forefathers." To some this may sound irrational and nebulous. Yes, fog it is, fog indeed—but that stormy, whirling fog out of which new worlds are being born.

Darius Milhaud's Service Sacré is not of the same stature as Bloch's work, although more liturgical in its general attitude. Milhaud wins new honors for the melodic lilt of the Southern French tradition which he dyes in the colors of his often cliché-ridden polytonal harmony. A perfectly delightful number is to be found in the appendix which contains pieces for the Sabbath Eve Service. *L'cha Dodi,* in spite of its easygoing, mechanical form emerges utterly disarming by its feminine grace.

In my own work I am dedicated to the task of formulating my musical ideas with as much plasticity as my talent will allow. My style may be described as a contemporary polyphony, by no means atonal, but at times pushing the borders of tonality toward their limits. Having steeped myself in Jewish melos, both Occidental and Oriental, I am not consciously striving for Jewishness. I have acquired an innate trust that the pilot light is alive and will kindle the flame when I am calling for it.

Of the composers discussed so far, nine are not alive anymore: Achron, Hugo Adler, Binder, Bloch, Freed, Helfman, Jacobi, Saminsky and Weinberg. The others are either middle-aged or older men. Few composers of the younger generation have shown a more than passing interest in the music of the Synagogue. But I will name three who have distinguished themselves in the field.

Samuel Adler, son of the cantor-composer mentioned

above, has contributed several complete Services as well as a number of anthems and responses. His *Shir Chadash* (A New Song) for cantor, three-part choir and organ, and *Shiru Ladonai* (Sing Unto the Lord) for solo voice and organ, were mainly created in answer to practical needs and offer excellent examples of *Gebrauchsmusik* on a high level. I am particularly referring to *L'cha Dodi, Veshamru III* and *Yismechu I* in *Shir Chadash,* and *L'cha Dodi* and *Barechu* in the solo Service. Adler's most sustained effort is a Sabbath Service *B'sha-arey Tefillah* (Within the Gates of Prayer), for cantor, mixed choir and organ. The style is freely polyphonic and characterized by sudden shifts of the tonal center. Example No. 3, taken from the *K'dushah* for the Sabbath Morning Service, shows the composer's skill and imagination.

Charles Davidson, cantor in a conservative Synagogue, must be counted among those cantors who have achieved a thorough professionalism as composers. He is a versatile musician writing dissonant harmony ("The Earth is the Lord's"), traditional music of East-European origin, brightened by cautiously enriched harmony ("Hashkivenu"), jazz and simple accompaniments to folk tunes ("Saenu"). I am not convinced when he mixes styles in one and the same piece, as in "The Earth is the Lord's" where we get a passage like Example No. 4, as against a conventional ending in Example No. 5.

A choral number from Davidson's "Dialogue with Destiny", called *Vaya-ar v'hiney hasneh* strikes me as a fully realized composition, even if the music is not in agreement with the miraculous scene of the Burning Bush. Here, a simple, fairly diatonic vocal line is set against a piano accompaniment of greatly refined rhythm. The rhythmic element appears as the contemporary feature of an otherwise traditional composition. Since Davidson's sensitivity to rhythm seems more highly developed than his ear for immovable rightness of dissonant harmony, a satisfying work emerges.

Yehudi Wyner has not yet written in quantity for the Synagogue but his two works, a Friday Evening Service and a Torah Service for Sabbath Morning, are original and challenging enough to warrant some detailed remarks. Of the two works, the shorter Torah Service, scored for cantor, mixed choir, two trumpets, one horn, one trombone and string bass,

is more unified stylistically although its predominantly
chromatic complexity may be less idiomatic for the Synagogue.
The earlier work requiring cantor, mixed choir and organ, is
preceded by a foreword in which the composer states some of
his aims. "I tried to create an expression of directness and intimacy, relevant to the modest, undramatic conduct of worship
in the traditional Synagogue" and further "traditional fragments have been used in a very free way, but the
traditionalism of the Service stems more from absorbed experience than applied method."

The first statement referring to the intimacy of the Service is borne out by the work but it is also apologetic in the
sense that Wyner is aware of his limitations. At moments when
the text demands drama, such as in *Hashkiveynu* ("Remove
from us every enemy, pestilence, sword, famine and sorrow")
the music offers no more than primitive shouts in octaves.
Another instance: the tumultuous verses of Psalm 96 ("Let the
sea roar and the fulness thereof, let the fields exult and all
that is therein; then shall all the trees of the wood sing for
joy") are rendered in a stationary, soft repetition of a short
phrase. This might be interpreted as an expression of awe but
it is hardly a musical equivalent of the unrestrained exuber-
ance of the text.

The remark about the role of tradition gives the key to
Wyner's approach. The Service is indeed a transformation of
traditional motifs, from strict adherence to creative remodeling. The most conspicuous motif occurring again and again is
the *Tipcha* motif, one of the 28 *ta-amey han'ginot* (neumes) used
for the chanting of the scriptures (Example No. 6). Idelsohn's
collection of the chants of Oriental Jewish communities is used
in *Aleynu* and the Benediction. The problem of an organ accompaniment for *Aleynu* is solved delicately by one sustained
chord which represents in a vertical column the notes of the
melody. The reason why, after this, the *Vaanachnu* section is
written as an unaccompanied unison does not become clear.

The short organ pieces seem to me the most prob-
lematical part of the Serivce. The composer is fully conscious
of it when he says in the preface "The organ pieces are clearly
different from the rest of the music. They should be regis-
tered and paced to give the illusion of being in a world apart."
That the organ pieces are not integrated is obvious; they stand

by themselves, locked out and shivering. My impression is that Wyner, for some reason or other, does not like the organ for Jewish worship, and allows this feeling to come to the surface. Significantly, this problem does not arise in the Torah Service which is not accompanied by organ but by five instruments.

The separateness of the organ, however, is not observed with absolute strictness. There are quite a few places where organ music intrudes into the vocal writing, not as subservient accompaniment but in independent preludes and interludes. Then we may get a clash of styles, as in Example No. 7, where a finely balanced modal unison passage is followed by an organ interlude which is incomprehensible in this context. The situation of the organ in juxtaposition with the choir is overcome with conspicuous success in the case of *Lecha Dodi* where a complete integration is achieved.

In spite of all these exceptions, Wyner's work is an important contribution, not only by virtue of its genuine and unmistakably Jewish flavor but also by the contemporary, urbane treatment given to the material by a cultivated and unconventional musician.

In conclusion, I would like to touch upon an uncomfortable question brought about by the title of this essay which uses the term "contemporary." Naturally, in a literal sense, all music written by contemporary composers is contemporary music. Narrowing the question to the point I wish to make, we should phrase the question like this:
—How contemporary, meaning how advanced, how modern, can Synagogue music
—or, for that matter, Church music—be?

The works of the younger composers discussed here as well as my own contributions are certainly progressive in comparison to what has gone before. Although often dissonant, they are still within the bounds of tonality, and not committed to the school of atonal writing.

I do not believe that it is a matter of practical considerations which detains composers from writing atonal music for the Synagogue. There seems to be a natural, probably even a historical, instinct at work which recognizes that only a style that has already gained general acceptance will be possible in a house of worship.

Much of the progressive, though tonal, music written for

the Synagogue must still wait its turn. Even a neo-classical
work like Stravinsky's Mass, written nearly twenty years ago,
has not yet taken root in the Catholic Church where it belongs, and to this day has remained a concert work Schönberg's atonal Psalm 130, dating from the year 1950, was written
in Hebrew and meant for the Synagogue. It may be found in
an Anthology of Jewish Music but, to my knowledge, has not
yet been heard in our sanctuaries. Thus, the term "contemporary", as used for this article, means "progressive" in the
relative, and necessarily conservative, sense of Church History.
It does not apply to what currently goes as the last cry of
avant-garde composers.

Example No 1

Tov l'hodos

Allegro maestoso

LAZARE SAMINSKY

Herbert Fromm

L'cho Dodee

Example No 2

Schalit

Example No 3   Samuel Adler

Example No 5   Charles Davidson

Example No 6   Wyner

Example No 7   Wyner

THE TETRAGRAMMATON IN MUSIC

(An Imaginary Discourse Preceding the Playing
of Ernest Bloch's *Sacred Service*)

Speaker:

As previously announced, I'll speak tonight about the Tetragrammaton in Music. That such a theme would interest only a few people is something I fully expected. Thus, it is easy for me to avoid the trap laid for so many speakers when facing a small audience: Scolding those present for those who did not come.

I shall even abstain from calling you "a special audience." If I did, I'd be falling into another trap. What sounds like flattery of the audience turns out to be self-adulation of the speaker who assumes that only "a special audience" could appreciate his message.

Having disposed of these more obvious traps, we are ready to turn to our theme which specifically considers Ernest Bloch and his Sacred Service *Avodat Hakodesh.* Its initial six notes

are heard throughout the work, and are even marked by brackets to show their importance whenever they occur.

The first four notes are elementary, known for centuries as *cantus firmus* for counterpoint exercises, and used for their highest purpose as the opening statement of the Finale to Mozart's *Jupiter* Symphony.

47

The Tetragrammaton, being the most sacred, unspeakable name of God, has only four letters in its unvoweled Hebrew spelling: *Y H V H*, whereas our motif comes to six notes.

Still, I think that those six notes are a representation of the Tetragrammaton—not in its Hebrew spelling but in its transliteration: *YAHWEH*. However, there is a problem that must be solved if my interpretation is to hold up.

In the six letters of the transliteration, the third and the sixth letters are the same. Not so in Bloch's motif, where the identical notes occur in the second and fifth place. Why this discrepancy in what I take to be an instance of musical symbolism?

To explain why Bloch could not allow his six notes to correspond exactly with the transliteration of the Tetragrammaton, I must present some theological and historical facts.

The Third of the Ten Commandments reads:

> Thou shalt not take the name of the Lord Thy God in vain; for the Lord will not hold him guiltless that taketh His name in vain.

This law had consequences of which I shall give some examples.

1. The Bible tells us that the Most Holy Name of God could only be pronounced once a year by the High Priest on *Yom Kippur*, the Day of Atonement.
2. When the Tetragrammaton appears in prayer or scripture, Jews unanimously pronounce it *Adonai* (Lord) and even change it to *Adoshem* in secular use.
3. Another name of God, *Elohim*, may be pronounced in prayer. But the fear of the Third Commandment is such that orthodox Jews change *Elohim* to *Elokim* if the word is used outside of prayer.
4. Even in English, religious Jews spell God as G-d to make sure not to be in conflict with the Commandment.

This brings us back to Bloch. His deliberate change in the six-note motif was, in my opinion, caused by obedience to the Third Commandment and the Jewish practice following that Law.

Voice from the audience:
  I just cannot believe that Bloch made his choice for such reasons. I don't even think he was faced with a dilemma. Your thoughts never occurred to him, he simply took his motif as a composer who saw in it possibilities for elaboration.

SPEAKER:
  However we look at it, we can say with certainty that the constant use of the six notes is not accidental. There can be no doubt that Bloch had something special in mind. He is dead, we cannot ask him anymore. Even if he were here to tell us, we could not be sure that his answer was to be taken as Absolute Truth. A composer of his type works by unconscious, perhaps even atavistic, impulses that rarely surface as reflection and thought. This leaves us with speculation.
  Your simpler, more practical answer, has much to recommend it. Yet, I am not willing to abandon my chain of thought, which may be called a Talmudic approach to music. But it could well be that, by combining the two interpretations, we may be touching the hem of truth—a modest claim indeed.

Short Pause.

No audience reaction.

Speaker:
  In spite of my ready compromise I still see doubt on your faces. Under these circumstances, the best I can do is seeking shelter under the last paragraph of a fantastic story by Nicolai Gogol, the Ukrainian-Russian writer of the early 19th century:

  > "Nevertheless, in spite of all, and although one may admit this, that and the other, and perhaps even. . . . Well, where in the world is there no nonsense? Whatever you may say against this story—there is something to it. Think what you will—such things occur. Rarely though. But they do occur."

THE MEANING OF WORSHIP TO THE ARTIST*

It would be difficult for me to describe, even in the most general outlines, the role of the arts in a divine Service. I am grateful to be relieved of dealing with too many aspects, and I welcome the opportunity to say in personal terms, and as a composer, what the act of worship means to me. PRAYER AND RITUAL—The Word and the symbolic Act.

THE WORD:

I am stirred in a particular way by the content and poetry of our devotional literature, not in a literary sense alone, but by an additional dimension which, for me separates Bible and Prayer from other works of literature which, on a different level, I may hold in abiding love and admiration. It is this extra dimension which extends the borders of literature to a commitment that binds me to a historic continuity and its countless facets.

THE RITUAL:

The one act which, after many years of weekly Services, never fails to run a shudder down my spine, is the taking of the Torah from the Ark. This, our Pageant of Fidelity, celebrates a scroll of parchment, clothed in velvet, crowned with silver and sounding with tiny bells as it is carried from the shrine to the desk. We revere the Word, no face, no saint—only letters. But letters we associate with a remote event of Divine Revelation.

Such is the soil on which my imagination thrives. What I want to capture in my music is the pride and majesty of a

---

*This paper was given at Temple B'rith Kodesh, Rochester, New York on March 2, 1968.

faith which, as an indestructable substance, survived the tor-
tures of history.

This explains why my music does not foster the "Ghetto
tone" which in the popular mind is the sum of Jewish music. I
know quite well that the experience of persecution had to find
a reflection in music and literature, and that genuine creations
have resulted from this theme. I personally am not drawn to
this preoccupation with suffering and have chosen—or rather
am compelled by my natural reactions—to make the Trans-
cendence of our faith the center of my work.

From this basic position I would now venture to remark
on some aspects of Synagogue music in our day. I do not believe that the vogue of Chassidic music which in recent years
has had an impact on the American Synagogue is a desirable
and promising development. The music of the Chassidic
movement is entirely linked with a way of life, with an
ecstacy of prayer and dance which cannot be transferred
successfully to another climate and civilization. When Chassidic melodies are severed from their environment and original purpose they lose their value and turn into quite ordinary
music. Those of us who do not live the Chassidic life—and
this is the majority of American Jews—cannot hope to capture
in Chassidic music the spirit which once illuminated these
melodies. All that is left to us is the modest setting of a ring
whose stone got lost as it was passed from hand to hand.

A word about jazz and rock services which have cropped
up in many places throughout the country. The simplistic
level of these Services cannot satisfy an ear steeped in the
music of Bach and Bloch. I, by upbringing and inclination,
must confess that I cannot find a personal relationship to jazz
and rock. Of one thing I am sure: If the young people want
to do "their own thing" they should do it all the way and set
to work writing new prayer texts. They must not fall back on
the words of the traditional prayer book which cannot be
forced into the same yoke with the kind of music the young
generation prefers. The printed statement of the composer of
a Rock Service to the effect that Church music, through the
influence of jazz and rock, is now entering its greatest period,
is utter nonsense, no matter from what angle we look at it.

In our *Havdalah* prayer which is the bridge from Sabbath

to weekday we find the phrase *Hamavdil beyn kodesh l'chol* "He who distinguishes between the Holy and the Profane," meaning here the separation between the Sabbath and the week of labor. One can hardly contest the statement that jazz and rock are secular idioms. As such, they should not find a permanent place in Synagogue or Church where we are supposed to close the door to wordly pursuits.

The argument has been heard that in former centuries secular music also crept into the Church and has stayed there ever since. This is true but two points should be considered: The popular tunes of that time had intrinsic musical value and the composers taking them into the Church clothed them in the splendid brocade of a highly developed art. What emerged was nothing less than the chorale settings of Johann Sebastian Bach.

Yet, based on this historic evidence, I will not deny the possibility that in the hands of a good and sensitive composer certain traits of today's popular music—not necessarily its melodic elements—may be integrated into a liturgical style of the future.

Surely, the Synagogue composer, no less than any other composer, must be concerned with the relevance of his message. But who can define relevance? Our basic prayers may serve as examples, if not as definition. Their broad human content poured into the asbestos-mold of durable language has withstood the fires of our changeable history throughout the centuries. I am not sure that anyone today can produce such solidity in music. Be that as it may: A liturgical composer must not allow himself to be pulled down by the leveling tastes of the masses. He should remember a commandment seen as inscription on many of our Torah shrines:

Da lifney mi attah omeyd
Know before whom you stand.
Five words. Five fingers of a pointing hand.

THE IDEAS AND GOALS OF MY
SYNAGOGUE MUSIC*

A composer faced with the task of explaining the ideas and goals of his work finds himself in an ambivalent position. On the one hand he is glad that there are people interested enough to hear about it, on the other hand he is aware of the inadequacy of words expected to elucidate a language which is self-sufficient and should not be in need of translation.

In poetry, relatively few penetrate to its core although every word of the poem may be known to the reader. The constellation of words, their hidden meanings, the long shadows behind metaphors, are the substance of the poem but they will not speak to an unsympathetic or casual reader.

In the case of music we are dealing with an even more elusive language. Its vocabulary is fluctuating, its grammar changeable and subject to innumerable amendments. Yet, in spite of this, music—no matter how boldly the composer may handle his material—is a powerful means of communication between man and man, the laws of an esoteric constitution revealing themselves step by step as the piece unfolds.

Having said all this as a precautionary introduction, I shall proceed with the theme of this symposium.

As a composer of Synagogue music I am trying to gain a fresh, elemental approach by surrendering myself to the impact of the text. I have an ear for the inflection of the language and the poetry of its images. Words mean a great deal to me and spur me on to search again and again for a musical phrase more apt perhaps than the one that first came to

*This paper was read at a Symposium of the Jewsih Liturgical Music Society of America, on March 12, 1964, at Temple Emanuel, New York City.

mind. The wheels spin and turn and the act of creation begins.

Musical composition, however, when applied to the liturgy of worship, finds itself moving within certain limits which should not be overstepped if the work is to serve its purpose. Synagogue music has to fulfill a function and should be more than a rhapsodic outpouring.

I shall not try here to do the impossible and give a full answer to the question: What makes a piece of music liturgical? Among desirable features I would mention a satisfying interpretation of the text, unburdened by an overdose of emotion, a lucid musical texture and a length properly designed for the place a piece should occupy within the overall structure of the service. May I add that with the latter point I am not advocating the bald utilitarianism of the so-called "practical" service music widely used in our Synagogues.

These, in general terms, are some of the guide posts in approaching the task. But generalities are not enough. A composer writing his music is dealing with a host of particulars, the most important being the choice of his material. Here the fundamental question arises: tradition as against free creation. Old wine in new bottles, meaning traditional modes in modern garb, or new wine in new bottles, meaning independent melodies in contemporary settings.

I have gone both ways. When using traditional modes I reserve the right of musical selectivity since not all traditions are of equal merit. The *Ahava Rabba* mode, with its taint of self-pity, appears sparingly in my work, no matter how much the interval of the augmented second may appeal to he nostalgia of the congregants.

The study of Idelsohn's collection of Hebrew-Oriental melody has been beneficial to my work. The chants of the Near-East come close to my ideal of liturgical melody: supremacy of the text, idiomatic inflection and a simplicity of expression which corresponds with the linguistic cast of our prayers.

Remolding this type of melody for use in our Synagogues presents a challenge to the contemporary composer, demanding flexibility and a resourcefulness for which no models exist. The repetitious brevity of Oriental motifs leaves much room for the composer's imagination. He must mobilize his creative powers if a satisfactory piece of music is to emerge from the mere hints of the original. The cultivation of this material will add a new dimension to our musical heritage and may become a link between the Oriental and Occidental segments of our people.

Another melodic tradition which has held my interest is the Sephardic music, as preserved in Frederico Consolo's collection published in 1891 in Italy. Here we find enchanting stretches of serene melody, unmistakably European in cut and phrasing, but most uncommon in their application to Jewish worship.

I have incorporated some of this material in my Organ Suite, a work planned with the idea of bringing several traditions together under one roof, by which I mean the stylistic unity of a consistent musical approach. Of the six movements, three use Sephardic sources, two Ashkenasic material and one an Israeli folksong.

In those works of mine which do not use specific motifs of a given tradition it sometimes happens that the melodic contours fall into the general type of those traditions which I admire most, so that a synthesis emerges between tradition and the free creative impulse. There is a saying that after many years of married life an actual resemblance of features may develop between two partners. It seems even more likely that something of the sort could occur in the realm of artistic creation.

A word about modernism in Synagogue music: it is historically true that sacred music never was a vehicle for experimentation. The Church music of Bach, for instance, was contemporary in the sense that it wrapped up the firm stylistic possessions of a period in transition, but it was not revolutionary.

This led to the curious situation that Bach was attacked by the younger generation of composers as being too conservative in his contrapuntal writing while at the same time the Church reprimanded him as being too complicated. He was told that it was difficult for the congregation to sing with his playing of hymns, the very same settings which we today consider the most perfect examples of their kind. Thus he found himself stoned by both camps. We have no Bachs in our midst but the Jewish composer who does not wish to continue in the vein of Sulzer, Lewandowski and Gerovich, yet is not willing either to write atonal music for the synagogue, may find some comfort in the similarity of the situation.

It is not easy to acquire enough self-confidence to disregard the contemptuous shouts from the left as well as the restraining exhortations from the right. In my work I adhere to no particular musical theory. Quartal Harmony, Twelve Tone System, Pure Diatonicism—none of these can force me into their exclusive service. I prefer the freedom of choice and with it the pain of always new decisions.

There is no denying that I have been criticized for being concerned too much with matters of style. In our time which by its very nature cannot grant style as an inherited birthright, each composer must struggle to clarify his means of expression. He must conquer the ground he stands on if he wants to own anything at all. I cannot know if my labors will bring durability to my works but I am convinced that my efforts for consistency of style, for intellectual cleanliness, are rooted in a layer much deeper than mere aestheticism.

Finally, I need not remind you that the ideal picture of what Synagogue music should be in its weekly practice is realized only on rare occasions. The rift between reality and ideal will always cause us a measure of distress. But in the face of congregational, and often rabbinical, resistance we must be content with slow progress and learn to rejoice in every forward step.

As a composer, I am free and cannot be forced to compromise my ideals. As a practical musician working for the Synagogue, I cannot get my way all the time without yielding ground here and there. Whoever is not willing to pay this price would be well advised to abandon the field.

I prefer to remain at my post hoping that the limited good I can do within my own sphere may prove to be of some value. There is many a time when we are called upon to fight for our cause and it must be done. We are not salesmen in a department store where the customer is always right, but musicians in the service of divine worship. The Master demands that we do our part.

JEWISH MUSIC—IDEAS AND HOPES*

Prophecy is not my field, but I can speak about my hopes for the future. Anyone acquainted with my music will agree that I am not a backward composer. I find it necessary, however, to take a stand concerning certain contemporary fashions that have been riding the crest for some time. I am speaking about Rock and Jazz Services, electronic experiments and the like. These trends have the day and with it a perishable success, but I doubt that they are the prelude to a viable future.

Musically, I see a regression into banality mixed with a commercialism that has its eye on the barometere of public caprice. "Counter-Culture" and "Generation Gap" are the current slogans. They are slogans but not answers. I have no quarrel with the term "Counter-Culture" as long as I read it as meaning "against culture," which I consider an apt description. The generation gap is nothing new, it has always existed. The difference is that our young generation is noisier about it than preeceding generations.

I take the position that there is such a thing as musical standards, based on objective criteria. The Synagogue must find its way back to its calling, discard the idols of entertainment and discover again what gifted and thoughtful contemporary composers have created in the past decades. We need not only idealistic synagogue musicians but also rabbis who can see beyond the present day and are not ready to open the doors of our sanctuaries to every whim of the moment. This, I

*This article appeared in the Jewish Welfare Board's magazine *The Circle* in the winter issue 1971-72.

believe, belongs to the function of the Synagogue as a *Bet Hamidrash*, a House of Learning and Education.

Continuing this thought I cannot let the opportunity pass without taking issue with statements made by Dr. Hugo Weisgall in "Jewish Music Notes" of June 1971. He is quite right that Jewish music, by and large, is of medicore quality but his suggestions for a remedy are off the mark. Specifically, I disagree with two points of his presentation.

1) The question "What is Jewish Music?" has not been solved by the establishment of the State of Israel. The Jewish composer who writes Jewish music of a distinctly national character has not appeared so far. If he ever will is a matter of conjecture.

2) Commissioning composers like Copland, William Schuman, Wolpe, Rochberg and Kirchner is no guarantee to obtain that particular quality the Synagogue needs—if liturgical music is what we are talking about. The fact that they are Jewish and good composers fulfills only part of what is required. These men have made their reputation in the broad field of general music and, with an adequate commission, may be coaxed into writing a work of liturgical intent. But if any of them would deliver something of value to the Jewish community is another matter, even if we take a long view and are not concerned with immediate success.

Let it not be said that the Jewish community does not occasionally give a commission to a well-known composer for an auspicious moment, such as the Convention of the Central Conference of American Rabbis. But I recall with dismay that in one instance the recipient was a jazz composer who dabbles in sacred music.

I have no reason to suspect Hugo Weisgall of wanting big names for the sake of publicity. He is serious in his search for quality but, to my mind, moving in the wrong direction. The case of Ernest Bloch is different. True, his Sacred Service was a commissioned work but the commission went to him because earlier in his life he had already composed notable works on Jewish subjects. This cannot be said for the names Dr. Weisgall proposes, except, perhaps, for Copland and his early Vitebsk Trio, which as a type, had no progeny in Cop-

land's later output. Weisgall's utopia looks to me like a land
that has more monuments than people.

Shielding himself by calling his opinions a partisan view,
Weisgall must surely concede the same right to me, when I, as
a partisan of another persuasion, point to a respectable literature of Jewish liturgical music from the pen of modern composers who never made the "big time" but in their quiet corners, and without fanfare, have contributed to Jewish culture
in a truly significant way. What they have done happens to
conform with Dr. Weisgall's statement about Schönberg:
"What is good need not necessarily be popular."

THE ORGAN IN JEWISH WORSHIP*

A primitive reed organ was already known in the First Temple by the Hebrew term *Ugav*. The Talmud, referring to the practice of the Second Temple, calls it one of the two instruments retained from the First Temple (the other one being the *Shofar)*, and informs us further that it became defective and could not be mended. Another, more complicated type of organ, called *Magrepha*, was used extensively in the Second Temple, mainly for signal purposes. We do not have a satisfactory description but, by inference, we can imagine something like a pan pipe operated by mechanical wind pressure. A talmudic tractate speaks of ten holes, each of which could produce "ten kinds of songs," so that the instrument in this unlikely description was capable of yielding one hundred "kinds of songs."

Contrary to a rabbinic edict, banning instrumental music from the Synagogue, after the destruction of the Second Temple in Jerusalem, we hear of sporadic appearances of organs and other instrumnts, long before the Reform Movement raised the question early in the 19th century.

The introduction of an organ in the first Reform Synagogue built by Israel Jacobson in Seesen, Germany, in 1810, aroused a storm of indignation which grew to fierce dimensions when big cities, such as Berlin and Hamburg, also installed organs in their Temples. The *Orgelstreit* (organ quarrel), as it is known in German-Jewish history, divided congregations and produced a whole literature of rabbinical Responsa. The opposing parties founded their argument not only on the old injunction that instruments must not be heard

*This article appeared in *The Jewish Advocate*, Boston, on March 16, 1967.

63

in the Synagogue, but they also considered the use of the organ as infringing on the prohibition to imitate alien cults (*Chukkot hagoyim*).

Among the early Reform Temples was one, built around 1815 by the wealthy banker Jacob Herz Beer in Berlin. Beer's son, later world-famous as the opera composer Giacomo Meyerbeer, arranged the music for his father's temple. Enlightened a musician as he was, he did not wish to introduce an organ in Reform worship. "I consider it my merit," he wrote in a letter to the Jewish Community in Vienna, "that in accordance with Mendelssohn-Bartholdy, I arranged in Berlin an *a capalla* choir only. A man in prayer should approach God without any intermediary. The Jews have maintained that opinion since the destruction of the Temple, and we should not introduce any innovation. But, if instruments are required, then flutes and horns should be used, similar to those used in Solomon's Temple. However, the human voice is the most moving." Meyerbeer, obviously after consultation with Mendelssohn, gave a clear opinion but he was wrong when speaking of flutes in Solomon's Temple. The flute, *Chalil*, was considered a secular instrument and as such was not allowed in worship.

A writer and scholar of such high artistic sensibility as Leopold Zunz (1794-1886) seemingly liked instrumental music in the Synagogue, but made a conciliatory statement in his *Gottesdienstliche Vorträge* (Lectures on Worship): "Only the accompaniment of the music is new—but not un-Jewish. Instruments and song were a main part of the ancient Temple worship. . . . . but then, concord is the best sounding harmony and organ and choir should not be instituted if they cause a rift within the congregation."

After the dispute had settled the organ became a permanent and necessary part of Reform worship. Even a number of Conservative congregations decided for an organ although the instrument, in many cases, was looked upon with suspicion and not allowed to take part in all the Feasts of the Jewish Year. The first organ in an American synagogue was installed in 1841 in Charleston, South Carolina. Other congregations followed in quick order.

The instrument's most important function in the service

is, of course, providing an accompaniment for the singers. Solo music for organ in the synagogue is relatively new and no older than about one hundred years. The only worthwhile organ work on Jewish themes coming out of the 19th century is the *Fünf Fest Präludien* (Five Festival Preludes) by Louis Lewandowski, op, 37. No. 1 for *Rosh Hashana* is based on the *Barechu* motif, No. 2 for *Yom Kippur* on the *Kol Nidrey* melody, No. 3 for *Sukkot* on the *Hallel*, No. 4 for *Pessach* on *Addir Hu*, No. 5 for *Shevuoth* on the *Akdamut* tune.

Today we have a certain amount—not yet a literature—of solo music by Jewish composers written specifically for the synagogue. These pieces may be divided into two categories:

1) Larger, independent works based on Jewish motifs or written in a Jewish idiom, to be used either for recital purposes or as prelude and postlude material in the synagogue.

2) Strictly liturgical pieces in smaller forms needed during the reading of the *Kaddish* or other prayers.

A significant work is a volume of 42 pages, edited by Samuel Adler under the title *Organ Music for Worship* (Wallan Music, Inc., New York, 1964). This book, a collection of organ music by Jewish composers in America, contains pieces by Hugo Adler, Samuel Adler, Jean Berger, Herman Berlinski, A. W. Binder, Isadore Freed, Herbert Fromm, Ernest Levy, Heinrich Schalit and Robert Starer.

Among the volume's most extensive pieces I would name particularly Samuel Adler's "Feast of Weeks", utilizing three traditional melodies for *Shevuot*, and an imposing Passacaglia by Isadore Freed. I have special affection for a small organ prelude of only 13 measures, by Ernest Levy. It is called "The Sabbath Bride" and rests on a purely diatonic melody faintly recalling the chanting of *Shir Hashirim*, The Song of Songs. The melody is set forth with a minimum of accompaniment and is so finely stitched with melismatic ornamentation that it brings to mind the delicate work of Yemenite embroidery.

Aside from the volume discussed above, there is a considerable number of separate publications of organ music by Jewish composers, such as Samuel Adler, Ernest Bloch, Herman Berlinski, Mario Castelnuovo-Tedesco, Isadore Freed, Herbert Fromm, and Reuven Kosakoff.

In spite of what has been achieved so far, organ music for the synagogue is still a little known branch of Jewish music. It will grow in volume and stature and, at some future time, may well command the attention of the music world at large. In the works of Herman Berlinski I see the first steps in this direction.

THE INFLUENCE OF GERMAN-JEWISH COMPOSERS ON THE AMERICAN SYNAGOGUE*

The theme assigned to me for this Conference deals with the German-Jewish contribution to the American scene. I take it for granted that the term "German-Jewish" also includes the works of Austrian composers.

Proceeding in the customary order I should begin with *Salomon Sulzer.* Before doing so, allow me a short digression, for the sake of historic interest. Sulzer, born in 1804, was not the first Central-European composer of Jewish importance. He was preceded by *Ahron Beer,* born 1783, *chazzan* in Berlin, and one of the first cantors who, aside from a fine voice, possessed considerable musical knowledge. His manuscript of close to 500 numbers contains music for the holidays and 53 different services for Shabbat. The reason for this abundance of music for Shabbat is given in Beer's preface where he says among other things: "If a person hears a tune but once a year, it will be impossible for him to sing with the cantor during the Service, and therefore he will not be able to confuse the *chazzan.* It has become a plague to the *chazzanim* to have members of the congregation join the song." This remarkable statement is still worth quoting while we have to admit that Beer's influence on the American synagogue may only be found, if at all, in Orthodox worship.

Returning to Salomon Sulzer, we repeat what is common knowledge: the three volumes of his *Shir Tsion* are the first fully organized and artistic realization of musical settings

*This lecture was delivered at the "Conference on the Music of the American Synagogue," in New York City, on December 1, 1975.

for the liturgical year, exerting an unprecedented influence on the development of Western synagogue music. Sulzer, even today, is held in high esteem although much of his output is neglected in the American synagogue.

Eric Werner, in the preface to the 1954 edition by the Sacred Music Press, elucidates some of the causes for Sulzer's gradual disappearance. It is Werner's opinion that the most cogent reason may have been "a disinclination toward his music on the part of many East-European Jews who, often wrongly, considered it not in accordance with the musical tradition as they knew it."

Sulzer's choral numbers are generally in the German style of his time, and it is characteristic that the works he commissioned from non-Jewish Viennese composers fit in without a break. Franz Schubert's *Tov l'hodot* (a piece unworthy of the composer's genius) and Wilhelm Würfel's *Adon Olam* may serve as examples. Both compositions are still heard in our synagogues.

Sulzer's finely shaped, expressive recitatives, often indebted to the Polish tradition, still offer a rewarding experience. The *Hashkiveynu* (No. 39 in the *Arvit L'shabbat* section), written in the Phrygian mode, could be cited in place of innumerable other examples.

The famous Viennese critic Eduard Hanslick wrote a laudatory article on the occasion of Sulzer's 50th anniversary as a cantor. All of Vienna honored "den alten Sulzer" who—in Hanslick's terms—was one of the most popular musical personalities of Vienna.

Discussing the composer's *Shir Tsion*, Hanslick claimed to detect a Jewish-Oriental idiom throughout the work. The fact is that the choral numbers rarely show a Jewish birthmark, and it is surprising that a critic as learned and astute as Hanslick did not distinguish between Sulzer's recitatives and his choral music.

Our first musical illustration is Sulzer's *Avot*, the beginning of the *Amidah*. It is in the major mode and has the ring of authentic tradition. I used it in my Friday Evening Service *Avodat Shabbat*, with melodic and rhythmic modifications and with disregard of the bland accompaniment provided by Sulzer's son Joseph—well-known first cellist of the Vienna

Philharmonic Orchestra—who edited his father's work in the belated centennial issue of 1905.

(Example No. 1)

Next in line would be *Hirsch Weintraub,* born in 1817, son of Salomon Weintraub who, according to contemporary reports, was one of the great cantors in the history of Jewish music, and is still known by his nickname *Kashtan,* in reference to his red hair. Hirsch, also a cantor, turned into a composer of imposing skill. In his work *Shirey Beyt Adonai* he kept and reshaped many of his father's recitatives of distinctly East-European flavor. The choral pieces, in spite of Weintraub's Ukrainian extraction, show him a faithful follower of German music, as he knew and admired it in the works of Sulzer. Weintraub indulges in fugues, canonic writing and *cantus firmus* treatment of melodies, always with the sure hand of a professional composer. Yet, every time I open these pages I get a musty whiff of academic learning. The recitatives are genuine but in matters of harmony I cannot agree with Idelsohn who vastly overrates Weintraub's merit as an innovator.

It would be hard to determine how much of Weintraub's music is still alive in the American synagogue. Whatever the case, he is an important figure and perhaps the best representative of a Jewish liturgical composer who was comfortably at home in the traditions of East and West.

To a lesser extent, both in quality and quantity, something similar can be said of *Eduard Birnbaum* who succeeded Weintraub as cantor in Königsberg, East Prussia. The first part of his awkwardly titled work *Amanut hachazanut* is mostly ⋅filled with recitatives, the second volume offers extended choral pieces, generally simpler in texture than those of Weintraub. Birnbaum's *Hashkiveynu* is still a favorite with our cantors, in spite, or because, of its robust attempt at a dramatic interpretation of the text. As a musicologist, Birnbaum has a secure place thanks to his fine, sometimes pioneering, essays on different aspects of Jewish music.

Louis Lewandowski, born in 1821, is without doubt the most successful German-Jewish composer of Synagogue music. Sulzer notwithstanding, his hold over the European and

American synagogue was without rivalry in the late 19th century. Even to this day, much of his music has remained a staple in the repertoire of our synagogues.

What accounts for this favored position? The answer is fourfold.

First: a well-balanced mixture of traditional material with freely invented pieces,

Second: a musical craftsmanship not encountered in Jewish music since the days of Salomone Rossi in the early 17th century,

Third: for the first time in our history, the appearance of fully worked out organ accompaniments which in many instances do more than just duplicate the choral parts,

Fourth   and perhaps most importantly: a sweet and natural flow of melody schooled on the model of Felix Mendelssohn.

It is this latter point which in more recent times has brought forth criticism as to the Jewishness of Lewandowski's music. On this score, I recommend reading what Hugo Chaim Adler said in his introduction to the reissue of Lewandowski's High Holiday volume. "Lewandowski's style no longer finds universal acceptance. But a Jewish composer and his work must be judged by the standards of his time and the climate of opinion of his generation."

Here is a truth that also applies to the Jewish composers in our own time who for the past forty years have followed new stylistic trends, far removed from Lewandowski's ideals. No matter how free the contemporary Jewish composer may flatter himself to be, he cannot help being nourished by the musical environment in which he happens to find himself.

I have always found great pleasure in some of Lewandowski's stylized recitatives in his first publication *Kol Rinnah ut'fillah*, "The Voice of Song and Prayer." The second of the four settings of *V'shamru* has long been one of my favorites. As with all pieces in this volume, it is unaccompanied. I adopted the melody with slight changes and arranged it for cantor, choir and organ.

(Example No. 2)

Siegmund Schlesinger, born in 1835, came to America in 1860 and gained enormous popularity by filling the needs of the early Reform Movement. He provided complete Services for the official Union Prayerbook but his music will hardly be found today in the repertoire of self-respecting Synagogues. Without discrimination he wrote in the style of second or third rate opera, not even ashamed of putting Hebrew words under the music of Italian composers, such as Donizetti. But let it be said in Schlesinger's honor that he used the traditional tune for the High Holiday *Avot* and gave it a simple and sympathetic accompaniment in support of the voice.

A much more serious musician was *Edward Stark*, born in 1863, who was active as cantor at San Francisco's Temple Emanu-El. He introduced traditional motifs to the Reform Movement, especially in his High Holiday Services, showing himself an altogether capable composer. His music suffers from broad-shouldered pompousness and rhetorical gestures which are probably indicative of a sociological phenomenon: the economic flourishing of the American Jewish communities in the early years of this century.

When mentioning earlier new stylistic trends that have been pursued for the past forty years, I had especially one composer in mind who added a distinctive and novel voice to the music of the Synagogue. The man is *Heinrich Schalit*, a venerable composer, now approaching his 90th year. Having served in Munich as organist he was exposed to the music of the Synagogue's cantor-composer Emanuel Kirschner, a conservative follower of Lewandowski, dedicated to the preservation of the Southern German tradition. Challenged to seek new ways, Schalit gave up an already recognized career in the field of secular music, and began to write liturgical works. It turned into a sacred calling dominating his life to the almost complete exclusion of any other musical forms. His basic achievement called *Freitag Abend Liturgie*, appeared in Germany in 1933 and was revised and newly published in this country in 1951, under the title *Liturgiah Shel Leyl Shabbat*.

Schalit was the first composer of consequence to grasp the importance of the material accumulated by Avraham Zvi Idelsohn in his collection of Oriental Jewish chant. The imprint of these melodies, perfect in their lofty objectivity, permeates

Schalit's work, be it in direct quotations, such as *L'cha Dodi,
Tov l'hodot, V'ahavta, Y'varechecha,* or in the composer's own invention. Schalit's preference is clear but he did not neglect the
Ashkenazic tradition either, as shown in his settings of *L'chu
n'rannenah,* `Adonai malach* and *Vay'chulu.* It is significant that in
his preface Schalit speaks of "our ancestral memory," and I
see it at work when, without folkloristic models, the composer
must rely on the infallibility of that memory.

For all this melodic material Schalit avoided the harmonic
idiom of the 19th century, as exemplified by Lewandowski.
He forged his own langague, a tart diatonicism which he
treats in contrapuntal fashion, as in *L'cha Dodi,* or in
homophonic textures, tellingly dissonant, as in *Tov L'hodot.*

It strikes me as pertinent to observe that Schalit's name
turns out to be more than a coincidence. We pronounce it
Schálit (stress on the first syllable), but as a Hebrew word,
Schalít (stress on the second syllable) means Leader, Master.
We could hardly find a better name for a man who initiated a
stylistic change in Western Synagogue music and became a
Master of his craft. The second of our two examples is based
on a chant of the Babylonion Jews, as recorded by Idelsohn.

(Examples No. 3 and No. 4)

Heinrich Schalit came to this country as a refugee from
the catastrophe that befell European Jewry in the fatal year of
1933. Other Jewish composers, devoted to the music of the
Synagogue, also arrived and added their talents to the rejuvenation of our liturgical music that was already in progress in
America.

Cantor *Hugo Chaim Adler,* a prolific composer, had a fine
sense of tradition and knew how to set his material in a modestly contemporary, truly liturgical, style. A typical example is
his *El maley Rachamim.*

(Example No. 5)

His son, *Samuel Adler,* enjoys a considerable reputation in
the field of general music, having composed in all forms, from

chamber music to symphony and opera. Still, Synagogue music is an important aspect of his oeuvre. As a small sample, we show his *Barechu* from a Service for solo voice, titled *Shiru Ladonai.*

(Example No. 6)

Julius Chajes, mostly known for his Hebrew songs, has written a slim volume of music for *Erev Shabbat,* consistent in style and of an all but vegetarian purity in matters of harmony.

Eric Werner has given us valuable music for the High Holidays, based on the Ashkenazic tradition, and excelling in finely wrought organ accompaniments.

Herman Berlinski owns the distinction of having created a sizable body of organ music which may well be the foundation of a new literature for Reform Worship.

Frederick Piket wrote a number of complete Services for Shabbat and Holidays. His one-page *Tsur Yisrael,* a fleeting moment of lyrical inspiration, shows him at his best.

(Example No. 7)

It would be a serious omission not to speak of *Arnold Schönberg,* Austrian composer of world fame. Baptized in his early years in Vienna, he later returned to Judaism as a fervent *Baal t'shuvah.* A letter written in 1932 to his friend and pupil Alban Berg shows his position: "I know perfectly where I belong. I have had it hammered into me so loudly and so long that only being deaf could I have failed to understand it. And it's a long time now since it wrung any regrets from me. Today I am proud to call myself a Jew."

Schönberg produced a number of important works on Jewish subjects: the opera "Moses and Aaron," an unfinished oratorio "Die Jakobsleiter" (Jacob's Ladder), the cantatas *Kol Nidrey,* and "A Survivor of Warsaw." Shortly before his death he contemplated a series of Psalms to German words of his own writing, but only one of them was finished. On commission for Chemjo Vinaver's Anthology he wrote a single work in Hebrew for the Synagogue: Psalm 130—*Mima-amakim*

Keraticha Adonai, From the Depths I have called Thee, Lord. It is an *a capella* work in six part writing, conceived in Schönberg's Twelve Tone idiom and, like all works of the composer, extremely difficult. Stressing the esoteric attitude of the work, Schönberg notated the voices in the old clefs that have not been used for more than a hundred years.

As things are at the moment, when guitar and simple-minded folksong imitations have conquered many a pulpit, the acceptance of Schönberg's music in the synagogue looks doubtful, as, for that matter, does the resurrection of a whole literature of contemporary music which now lies dormant, waiting for a new day.

At the beginning of this lecture you heard my recasting of material by Sulzer and Lewandowski. Allow me now to close with two pieces of mine, not drawn from other models. They are *V'ahavta* from my Shabbat Morning Service *Chemdat Yamim* and the sacred song "Grant us Peace", text from the Union Prayerbook. In both cases you'll notice a kinship with cantillation and prayer modes, not quoted verbatim, but recreated from that reservoir of our ancestral memory of which I spoke before.

(Examples No. 8 and No. 9)

Example No 1

OVOS I
For Tenor

Sulzer-Fromm

TCL 835-73

Example
No. 2

V'SHOMRU

For Cantor (Tenor or Baritone), Mixed Voices and Organ

Duration: 2 min.

After a Melody by
LOUIS LEWANDOWSKI,
freely transcribed by
HERBERT FROMM

Example No. 3

III. Sabbath Eve Service (ARVEES L'SHABBOS)

8. BOR'CHU

Slowly and solemnly
(*Introduction is optional*)

H. SCHALIT

★ The "Bor'chu" may also start here.

Example
No. 4

10. V' OHAVTO

H. SCHALIT

With fervor
Recit. * CANTOR

V'- o - hav-to   aye— A - do-noy   E - lo - he - cho

b'-chol l'- vo - v'-cho uv-chol naf-sh'-cho   uv-chol m'- o - de - cho.

V'- ho-yu ____   ha-d'- vo-reem ho-ay - lo— a - sher o - no-chee__

m'- tsa - v'- cho   ha - yom   al   l' - vo - vo - cho..

* Oriental mode, Source: A. Z. Idelsohn "Songs of the Babylonian Jews"

Example No. 5

Published upon the 10th Johrzeit of Hugo Ch. Adler, 1894-1955

EYL MOLEH RACHAMIM
FOR CANTOR, MIXED CHOIR AND ORGAN.

HUGO CH. ADLER

BOR'CHU

Example No 6

Samuel Adler

Example No 7

Dedicated to Alfred and Paul Fromm

Grant Us Peace

HERBERT FROMM

Example No 9

Grant us peace, Thy most precious gift, e— Thou e - ter - nal source of peace, and en - - a - ble our na - tion to be a mes - sen - ger of peace un - to the peo - ples of the earth.

COMPOSERS IN ISRAEL*

Composers in Israel may be seen in three divisions, according to the trends they are pursuing. Except for the youngest set, born in Israel, they are immigrants who brought with them the taste and training of their formative years in Europe.

There is the older East-European school, rooted in Jewish-Slavonic, and later in Oriental folklore. Early settlers, such as Yoel Engel, Israel Brandman and Yitzchak Edel may serve as examples.

The Central-European school prefers abstract musical forms. Erich Walter Sternberg, Josef Tal and Hanoch Jacoby could be named here. Biblical or generally Jewish subjects play an important part in their works but folklore is not a prominent feature.

The Mediterranean school struggles with the problem of creating a synthesis between Oriental and Occidental music. The initial step to elaborate Oriental folk material in European fashion has now been superseded by the writing of original music which absorbs the experience of Oriental music in more independent ways. The outstanding names in this endeavor are Paul Ben Chaim, Oedeon Partos and Uria Boscovich. Julius Chajes, a longtime resident of the United States, having spent only a few years in former Palestine, must also be mentioned. Some of his Hebrew songs are among the finest achievements uniting Oriental and European elements.

Remarkable altogether, as a rare phenomenon in the modern world, is the existence of new folksongs which, in

*This paper was read on April 11, 1961, at the New England Jewish Music Forum in Boston.

their best examples are no longer fashioned after European models. Especially some melodies by Zaira and Gorochov proved eminently successful, both as musical types and in their acceptance by the people. Songs such as Zaira's *Hineh achallelah* and *Ashrey ha-ish* or Gorochov's *Saleynu* are first rate melodic creations, and like all true folksongs, sufficient in themselves as unaccompanied music.

The experience of the European composer living and working in Israel is vastly different from the experience of the Polish composer Chopin in Paris, or the Protestant North German Brahms in Southern Catholic Vienna. These composers, in whatever European capital they might have found themselves, were surrounded by the familiar climate of a highly geared musical culture. The changed environment added flavor to their music but there was no need to search for new beginnings.

The European composer in Israel, especially in the early days, lived in a lean, frugal country where musical institutions had to be built up slowly and modestly. But—and this is more important—a composer transplanted from Europe to Israel could not simply continue what he had been doing before by shutting himself off from the aural and visual impressions of his new country.

If a national style is what the Israeli composers are striving for, a synthesis between East and West presents itself as the central problem. The considerable influx of Oriental Jews in the past few years, and with it the changed proportions of Israel's population, has served to sharpen the issues on all levels. Cultural amalgamation must be sought from both sides. It will be a slow and painful process and definitive results must not be expected for some time to come.

So much for a general outline. Allow me now to give you some personal impressions I received on my trip to Israel in October 1960.

I had the good fortune to spend some time with the composer Paul Ben Chaim. He lives in a medium-sized apartment building in the center of Tel Aviv. There is a notice posted at his door, in both Hebrew and English: "Please, do not visit me unless you have an appointment." This, the civilized outcry of a famous and often disturbed composer! I did have a previous appointment and was cordially received by a tall, gaunt man, bald, with a healthy complexion and wakeful eyes behind heavy glasses. After some preliminary phrases in Hebrew, Ben Chaim continued in a leisurely South German dialect. Born in Munich, his original name was Paul Frankenburger and he, like myself, was educated at the State Academy of Music in Munich. My senior by seven years, he was at the time of my studies already active as coach at the Bavarian State Opera. I had never met him before, and now in Tel Aviv we found occasion to reminisce about our years in the Bavarian capital. We also talked about our mutual friend, the composer Heinrich Schalit, who before 1933 was living in Munich as organist of the synagogue. Schalit had a decisive influence on Ben Chaim's Jewish career, and his decision to settle in Palestine.

The conversation later turned to my music and Ben Chaim showed interest in some of my published works. He suggested that toward the end of my stay in Israel an hour of my music should be given for an invited audience of professional musicians and that he, Ben Chaim, would contact Peter Gradenwitz to organize such a plan.

Next day I visited Dr. Gradenwitz in his office. He is a musicologist, composer and editor of Israeli Music Publications. After some search for the office, I finally discovered the emblem known to me from their publications: the Hebrew Letter *Mem*, obviously meaning *Musicah*, shaped in the form of a harp with seven strings filling out the curve. Dr. Gradenwitz, not only a fine scholar but also a man of worldly grace, made the necessary arrangements for the projected concert, which was to take place after my return from Jerusalem, Haifa and several excursions into the lower and upper Galilee.

During my stay in Jerusalem I contacted Shabtai Petrushka, one of the program directors of the State Radio *Kol Yisrael*, The Voice of Israel. The main building of the station is a fine, grey stone mansion, once owned by an Abyssinian princess. After I had been cleared at the gate by a soldier, I was led to the office of Mr. Petrushka, a round-headed, friendly man who, aside from some chamber music, has made a name for himself by orchestral versions of folk melodies. A servant brought *Caffeh Turki,* strong and very hot Turkish coffee which one must learn to drink from small glasses without handles. While I was trying to find the right spot for holding the glass, we enjoyed a rambling conversation about many topics. Mr. Petrushka wanted tapes of my music to be used on future programs. Later I was shown through the many rooms of the station, furnished with excellent, up-to-date equipment. From the flat roof of the building one has a superb view of the old city and surrounding hills. This was as close as I could get. Old Jerusalem is in Arab hands and Jews are not allowed to enter. As a last round, Mr. Petrushka took me to a rehearsal of the orchestra which is in full time employment by the radio station. They rehearse in the splendid YMCA building of the British mandate era, opposite the King David Hotel. The orchestra, not large, is fully professional, although not of the highest quality. They were rehearsing a cantata by Hanoch Jacoby ending in a vivid *Hora* with canonic devices. The chorus was too small to be effective. After the rehearsal, a young woman from the violin section greeted me by name. She comes from Boston and played some years ago at Temple Israel when I conducted my cantata "The Stranger."

On coming back to Tel Aviv, Dr. Gradenwitz called for me at the hotel for the late afternoon concert of my music. The event took place at an artists' club and was attended by composers, conductors, performers and critics. We sat informally at a long table where tea and cake were served. After Dr. Gradenwitz had introduced me I preceded the playing of the tape of my liturgical Service *Avodat Shabbat* by a short historical survey of Synagogue music, stressing the recent developments in America.

While the sacred melodies of Oriental Jewish communities are recorded and transcribed in scientific fashion by a department of the Hebrew University, Israel shows very little creativity in the field of Synagogue music. The religious leaders are not interested in new musical trends, hence the Israeli composers have no incentive to write for a Synagogue that shuns contemporary music. Although there are first rate compositions of Psalms and other sacred texts by Israeli composers, they have no place in their synagogues and are treated as concert material.

If I am not mistaken, my liturgical work was received with

interest but not with any particualr understanding of its place within the framework of American Synagogue music.

For a second item on my program I had chosen a secular work, the song cycle "The Crimson Sap." To facilitate the comprehension of the work, my wife Leni gave first a complete reading of the English poems by Jean Harper. The song cycle evoked a warm reaction from the professional audience. A question and answer period ended the hour.

Later, at night, I took a walk along the beach at Tel Aviv. The sea was calm and in the curve of the bay ancient Jaffa could be seen with its fragile minaret rising from a black mass of houses. Tel Aviv and Jaffa—modern Europe and the old Middle East facing each other, an ever present challenge to all who live in this extraordinary country. Her problems are new and unprecedented. Music surely is not the most pressing question for a new nation. Nevertheless, what happens in music will perhaps be an indication of what happens on mundane levels. The dark saying of antiquity: "If there is something wrong in music, something is wrong in the state" may again take on a very concrete meaning.

PART II

FOUR COMPOSERS

SALAMONE ROSSI*

Hashirim Asher Lish'lomo, this is the title of three volumes issued by the Jewish Theological Seminary of America, in cooperation with the Cantors Assembly, New York, 1973. The excellent project of a new and complete edition of Rossi's works for the Synagogue, initiated by Hugo Weisgall, chairman of the faculty of the Cantors Institute at the Seminary, was carried out by Fritz Rikko, assisted by Joel Newman and other musicologists, as well as Hebrew scholars, such as Milton Feist. The source was the original publication of 1623 which, according to the custom of the time, was not printed in score but only in parts, and is preserved at the *Liceo Musicale* in Bologna. It took twelve years (1953 to 1965) to complete this modern and definitive edition.

The three books, lavishly printed, offer essentially the following material:

Volume I (261 pages): Preface by Hugo Weisgall, Acknowledgements and explanation of procedures by the editor, Fritz Rikko, Facsimile of the original title page in Hebrew, Facsimile of a tenor part *(Eyn Keyloheynu)*, and twenty-four out of Rossi's thirty three Hebrew compositions.

Volume II (239 pages): nine double choruses, one for seven voices, the rest for eight voices.

Volume III (113 pages) does not contain any music. It presents the Hebrew prefaces in English translation, then on one page an "Outline of Events in Rossi's Life" giving hardly more than the years of publication of Rossi's music during his lifetime, and the generally as-

*This essay appeared in the June 1974 issue of *Journal of Synagogue Music*.

sumed dates of his birth and death (ca. 1570-ca. 1630).
A more detailed account of Rossi's life and time would
have been desirable. This may be found in Peter
Gradenwitz' *The Music of Israel*, chapter 6, p. 130 to
157, also, though less informative, in Naumbourg's edition of 1877, under the heading "La vie et les oeuvres
de Salomon Rossi." The "Outline" is followed by Joel
Newman's substantial essay on the style of Rossi's Hebrew music.

The next chapter first explains the transliteration
of the text, acknowledging Raphael Edgar's assistance, then
goes on to what is called in this book "Text Underlay", seemingly a literal translation of the German "Textunterlage." The
problem of fitting Hebrew script, which runs from right to
left, to music going in the opposite direction, was solved by
the Venetian printers of 1623 in a tentative way. As the facsimile of the tenor part of *Eyn Keyloheynu* shows, the word *Eyn*
is placed under the first note of the music, which must go
from left to right, while the word *Keyloheynu* stands under the
last notes of a complete musical phrase. The proper distribution of the syllables was given over to the singers or their
leader who obviously knew how to deal with such situations.

In modern Isreael, Hebrew texts are put, syllable by syllable, under their notes so that the complete Hebrew word cannot be seen as easily as in the old Rossi edition. The clarity of
textual distribution more than makes up for this deficiency.

Pages 65-67 point out the liturgical usage of the texts.
Then comes the facsimile of a page from a prayer book,
printed 1557 in Mantua. The refrain of this prayer, recurring
ten times, is *Hosha-anah* "please save (us)," a truly subtle cover
for p. 71-77, which is a list of mistakes and additions (Corrigenda
and Addenda). This list is not always clear and by no means
complete. If a new printing should ever come about, one
could think of other prayers preceding these pages, such as:
S'lach lanu, m'chal lanu, kaper lanu—bear with us, pardon us,
forgive us.

The English part of volume III ends with a selected bib-
liography and a page called "Rossi's Sacred Music in Modern
Editions." To my amazement, Isadore Freed's transcription of
Rossi's Music (Transcontinental Music Publications, 1954) is

not mentioned at all, although it is, as far as I can determine, the most widely used edition of Rossi's music. Freed set himself the task of adapting Rossi's music, in many instances, to different texts, as used on Shabbat Eve in the American Reform Synagogue. He did so with varying success and scored admirably with a charming *L'cha Dodi* drawn from Rossi's eight part setting of *Adon Olam.*

Warning: The *Sh'ma* in Freed's book is not a work by Rossi. Samuel Naumbourg's late 19th century edition of Rossi's Hebrew works states frankly that the *Sh'ma* is not found in Rossi's *K'dusha* which, in Naumbourg's opinion, conforms to the text of the Sephardic version. Naumbourg's footnote reads: "Le Schema Israel ne figure pas dans le Kedouscha de Rossi. Je l'ai composé *et ajouté* pour compléter l'oeuvre." Going through the new Rikko edition, one finds that other parts of the K'dusha are also missing in Rossi's setting. These sections, in Rikko's surmise, were probably chanted by the cantor. We cannot be sure and I am not equipped to decide if Naumbourg's or Rikko's explanations are correct. Comparing Naumbourg with Rikko, it turns out that not only the *Sh'ma* but also the other missing sections were supplied by Naumbourg who was bent on making Rossi's piece fit the Ashkenazic text. Naumbourg's additions (the threefold *Kadosh, baruch k'vod, ani Adonai,* etc.) are easily recognized as the work of another hand.

It is surprising that Freed accepted the Naumbourg *Sh'ma* and did not apply his general procedure of adapting Rossi's music to the text on hand. When I performed the Freed edition, I reconstructed a satisfactory *Sh'ma* by searching through Rossi's works and putting the *Sh'ma* under a strong musical phrase Rossi had composed for another text.

After this necessary digression, back to Volume III. Following page 92 one must turn to page 113 and read from right to left until one reaches page 93. These pages offer original Hebrew texts, beginning with a facsimile of the title page, then the composer's dedication to his sponsor, Moses Sullam; after that, a lengthy foreword by Leone de Modena, two dedicatory poems, presumably also by Leone, and finally de Modena's Responsum of 1605 (written eighteen years before the appearance of Rossi's music) defending the use of art

music in the Synagogue. Leone strengthened his defense by
short statements of four other rabbis. The very last Hebrew
text is a curious copyright notice, providing that nobody could
print or purchase this music, in whole or in part, without
permission of the author or his heirs, for a period of fifteen
years.

The Hebrew of all this prefatory material is kept in an
exalted, biblical style, full of direct allusions or quotations
from the Scriptures. One example, taken from the copyright
notice, may suffice. What today is phrased in the dry legal
terms of "All rights reserved," appears like this: "We, the un-
dersigned, decree by the authority of the angels and the
words of the holy ones, invoking the curse of the serpent's
bite. . . etc."

There can be no doubt that Rossi's approach to
synagogue music was revolutionary for his time. The Hebrew
title page states in forthright language "*Chadashah ba-arets*", a
novelty in the land, and the extensive foreword by Rabbi
Leone de Modena may well be interpreted as an apologia for
so daring a step.

Leone de Modena (1571-1648), though an unstable character, was a gifted and colorful personality: Hebrew scholar,
poet in Hebrew, Italian and Latin, musician, alchemist and
gambler, and in spite of his diverse interests, a recognized
rabbinic authority. Enough of a musician, he was an ardent
admirer of Rossi who, as director of music at the ducal court
of the Gonzagas in Mantua, enjoyed European fame.

Rossi, unswerving in his faith, signed himself as Salamone
Rossi Ebreo, and was twice exempt from wearing the yellow
badge. Urged by de Modena, he published his Synagogue
music in 1623 but historical events prevented his reform from
taking effect. The last of the Gonzagas died in 1630, and
Mantua, after a siege of seven months, was stormed and rav-
aged by Austrian troops. Most Jews fled and all traces of Rossi's life are lost in the upheaval of the time.

Rossi's work lay forgotten for two hundred and fifty
years, until another Synagogue composer rediscovered it. I am
speaking of Samuel Naumbourg who was born in 1815 in
Bavaria and died in Paris 1890, as cantor of the Temple Con-
sistorial. Under the sponsorship of Baron Edmond de

Rothschild he issued the Hebrew works of Rossi in 1887. Naumbourg's edition was out of print for a long time, until the Sacred Music Press of New York made it available again in a facsimile reprint, in 1954, with a preface by Isadore Freed. Naumbourg's enthusiasm and zeal to restore Rossi's music to the Synagogue, after a lapse of more than two centuries, was unusual for a man of the 19th century and deserves our full admiration. He had to overcome countless difficulties in his research, and without the sponsorship of Edmond de Rothschild, to whom the volume is dedicated, the project could hardly have been undertaken.

Naumbourg, a contemporary of Halévy and Meyerbeer, was very much a product of his time. Thus, his volume abounds in editorial liberties, clearly showing an attempt to smooth over what he considered harsh in Rossi's original. Here is one example to illustrate the point:

which is an insipid recasting of Rossi's

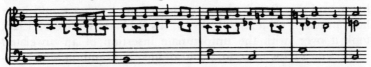

In many instances Naumbourg eradicated the freshness of the so-called "false relation," meaning the chromatic changing of a note not occurring in the same voice. I quote from the famous setting of Psalm 80. Rossi ends a phrase with a G major chord in this spacing:

and begins the next phrase, a B flat major chord

in this position:

In Naumbourg's transcription, the chord progression appears like this:

He obviously wanted to avoid the uncomfortable step of a diminished Fifth in the tenor.

A unanimous vote of gratitude must go to Naumbourg for transforming Rossi's five part setting of the *Kaddish* into *Adon Olam,* although Rossi's work contains an original *Adon Olam* for eight part double chorus. Naumbourg recognized that the *Kaddish* melody with its constant repetition (probably based on a traditional Sephardic tune?) would be ideal for a hymn and that Rossi's choral setting of the *Kaddish* would have little practical value. Saminsky, in his Sabbath Service of 1926, took it over, with the unfortunate insertion of an unrelated tenor solo of his own, and a grandiloquent ending which destroys Rossi's noble simplicity. Freed's version is generally better but he also could not resist the urge for an "effective" conclusion. *Adon Olam,* thanks to Naumbourg's keen eye, is today the best-loved and most performed of Rossi's works. Rikko's new edition made us aware of the astounding fact that Rossi did not write this music to the words of a hymn that occupies such an important place in our liturgy.

Taking a general view of Rossi's music, one may safely say that he had absorbed and mastered the best his time could offer, in his words, "the science of music." In professional terms: we are dealing with pure triads, both major and minor, and the diminished triad in its best sounding first inversion, all fitted into modal scales. These basic elements are imaginatively enhanced by passing notes, suspensions, anticipations, imitative entrances, etc. In matters of form, it is apparent that even long pieces are built by adding up short phrases, which in themselves come to complete cadences, and by repetition of whole sections. The range of the soprano *(canto)* is often low. Transposition is not always the answer since it may take other voices into an unwanted *tessitura*. It may be better to strengthen low soprano parts by adding mezzos and altos.

Rossi's craft is impeccable and it is fascinating to see how he avoids parallel Fifths by a sly crossing of voices. He can write an exquisite three part texture for *Bar'chu*, but is equally at ease with an eight part double chorus. His works for double chorus are harmonically simpler than those for three to six voices, relying on a monumental, homophonic style. We think of large spaces although the Synagogue in Mantua was probably a modest place compared with the cathedrals of the time. Rossi uses superb judgment, knowing exactly when to alternate the two choruses and when to bring them together in a full tutti.

Of particular interest is No. 33, a wedding ode, whose text may well have been supplied by Leone de Modena. The secularity of the words, religious connotations notwithstanding, is reflected in the music by playful echo effects of the second chorus which takes up, note by note, the ending phrases of the first chorus. It is a sort of dialogue where the wife (Chorus II) agrees with her husband (Chorus I), but the two also sing together (measures 115-131) and join for a radiant ending (measures 164-183). I cannot think of a more festive piece for a wedding ceremony. The text also has some striking turns. Our rabbis, speaking to bride and groom under the *chuppah*, always emphasize the strength derived from the sharing of grief. The old poem phrases it this way: "Protected as his own ewe lamb, she is silent though shearers come. He will come to honor her more than himself. Sheltered under his wing, she shall be lifted up high over his house."

A particular care for words or mood, as in this piece, is rare in Rossi's Hebrew works. There are, of course, some notable exceptions:

Psalm 137—the extraordinary, moving chord progression on the words *gam bachinu*, "there we wept,"

Psalm 118—the jubilant imitation, cascading through several voices on the words *nagila v'nism'cha vo,* "we will rejoice and be glad in it,"

Psalm 29—a violent insistence on a short motif, welling up in all six voices, on the words *vaishaveyr Adonai et arzey halevanon,* "the Lord breaketh the cedars of Lebanon."

But such details are exceptional. In *Hashkiveynu,* for instance, he makes nothing of the words *V'haseyr mey-aleynu oyeyv, dever, v'cherev, v' ra-av,* "remove from us every enemy, pestilence, sword and famine." Examples of disregard for specific words are so numerous that one may well call it a trait of Rossi's music. I suspect that this lack, in spite of Rossi's mastery, accounts for his modest place in the general history of music, as Weisgall puts it. The composer kept hiding behind the protective shield of his invulnerable technique.

Most writers on Rossi speak of a "pun" when discussing the title *Hashirim asher Lish'lomo* which is taken from the biblical *Shir hashirim asher lish'lomo,* the "Song of Songs, which is Solomon's." Rossi's title is the deliberate choice of a proud man, in full possession of his gifts, who had no reason to feel inferior when linking himself to a king. He was a king in music, and recognized as such. I prefer to read the title in this sense, and my interpretation is borne out by certain phrases in the composer's foreword and dedication:

"... the Lord, God... opened my ears and granted me the power to understand and to teach the science of music... to take the choicest of all as an offering... I did not restrain my lips but ever increased my striving to enhance the psalms of David, King of Israel... for discriminating ears... not for my own glory but for the glory of my Father in Heaven who created the soul within me. For this I will give thanks to Him for evermore."

For further elaboration, I am calling on Leone de Modena's remarks which instruct us in three important points.

1. Rising above the ghetto:

"A rainbow has appeared in our days in this man of knowledge who has written and engraved these songs of praise... after the splendour of the people of Israel had been dimmed by the passage of days and years, he restored their crown to its ancient estate as in the days of the Levites..."

2. Pride in the achievement of a Jewish musician whose
   work measures up in quality to that of the Gentile
   composers:
   "No longer will arrogant opponents heap scorn on the
   Hebrews, they will see that they too possess understanding, the equal of the best endowed."
3. Hope in a return to Zion where Rossi's songs would
   find their rightful place.
   "Life, prosperity and every joy to the author, until the
   Rock (God) returns His faithful ones to His restored
   sanctuary with songful lips."

Rossi's works for the Synagogue remained superior to
all that was written within three hundred years after him. I
am tempted to alter a sentence of Deuteronomy 34 (V'lo kam
navi od b'yisrael k' moshe) to read: "There did not arise in Israel
a composer like Salamon"—until the appearance of Ernest
Bloch and some chosen ones who prepared or followed his
ways.

A last word remains to be said about Hugo Weisgall's preface, found at the beginning of Volume I. I am not in sympathy with what Weisgall calls Rossi's "profound misapprehen-
sion of what the place of music is in a service as thoroughly
individualistic and egalitarian as traditional Jewish worship." It
is not quite clear to me what these phrases mean, but "misap-
prehension" is the wrong word. As pointed out before, Rossi's
approach was revolutionary and, as such, aimed against the
musical aspects of traditional Jewish worship. It was not mis-
apprehension but a probably unattainable, idealistic goal that
motivated Rossi. Rabbinical authorities, less enlightened than
Leone de Modena more often than not, put up a fence to
keep out new currents, fearing that assimilation and with it,
loss of Jewish identity, would ensue. This might be true in
other areas but our faith is hardly worth preserving, if artistic
excellence is seen as endangering it.

A depressing example of what I mean is of our own day.
Rabbi David Polish, president of the Central Conference of
American Rabbis, informed his colleagues of the Reform
Movement, in a newsletter of December 1972, that professional singers in the synagogue are questionable, and that the
role of the cantor should be no more than that of a song
leader for the congregation. An attitude like this, if observed,

would bring down the music in our synagogues to the level of trivial ditties and camp songs, burying, for who knows how long, an important literature created by Jewish composers who have devoted their talents to the enhancement of Jewish worship.

Weisgall says furthermore: "For the Jewish composer of the twentieth century, Rossi's example poses many significant problems still to be solved." I fail to see a problem in free composition for the Synagogue, if the composer draws on the best of his time, as Ernest Bloch did. I am not saying that *Nussach* and traditional modes should not be used. My decided preference goes to composers who in their works alternate free creativity, sparked by the text, with the use of traditional material which, in the hand of a true composer, acquires a new dimension. Only thus can our music match the literary quality of our prayers "for discriminating ears."

Stylistically, there can be no quarrel that Rossi's music is a product of the Italian Renaissance. How Jewish is it? The question of what constitutes Jewish music cannot be answered to everyone's satisfaction. Taking as the sole model what has come to us from the cantorial practice of Eastern and Central Europe is not enough. Without reservation, I say *Dayenu* when, as in the cases of Rossi or Bloch, a Jewish composer writes for a Jewish purpose.

Is there a synagogue musician who has not been exposed to the flea bite of a remark that music in the synagogue should not be a concert? At first blush, this sounds sensible but what is meant is in truth a demeaning of music. Nothing can be good enough to praise God on High, which, in musical terms, affirms that music in a house of worship should not lag behind the quality of a concert—with one important difference: Sacred music serves another purpose and good composers know it. Listening to artful music in church or synagogue can be a religious experience, but only if a congregation has been educated to this level of hearing. That such an education was in the minds of Rossi and Leone de Modena can be deduced from what they say in their prefaces and, most strikingly, from the music itself. As far as our present situation is concerned, I have every reason to despair of an improvement in the foreseeable future.

Weisgall's comparison of Rossi with Süsskind of Trimberg is not well taken. Süsskind, a *minnesinger* in the second half of the thirteenth century, was the only German poet of Jewish birth we know of in medieval times. Only six of his pieces are still in existence. They are completely in the style of his time, and the comparison with Rossi succeeds in this respect. But it breaks down in the matter of Jewish importance. Süsskind left nothing of any use to the Jewish community. This is not the case with Rossi whose works for the synagogue are resurrected in our day with increasing frequency.

I think it quite appropriate to take this miraculous phenomenon as an occasion to refer to another miracle quoted on the seal of the Jewish Seminary, and stamped on the three volumes of the new Rossi edition: *V'hasneh eynenu uchal*, "and the bush was not consumed."

A. W. BINDER: JEWISH LITURGICAL COMPOSER*
(1895-1966)

When I first came to this country, as a refugee musician from Germany, looking for work, I was sent to Rabbi Stephen S. Wise of the Free Synagogue. Dr. Wise, after having informed himself about my musical background, arranged a meeting with his music director, Abraham Wolf Binder. It was then that I met Mr. Binder for the first time. He received me warmly and invited me to his house where I played some of my music. His interest was aroused and he soon found work for me as rehearsal pianist and as organist in one of the concerts of the *Mailamm* (American-Palestine Musical Association), which later became the Jewish Music Forum.

After I had found steady employment as organist and choir director of Temple Beth Zion in Buffalo, Mr. Binder kept in touch with me and it was through his recommendation that in 1941 I was appointed music director of Temple Israel in Boston.

While studying in the summer of 1941 with Paul Hindemith in Tanglewood, Massachusetts, I again met Mr. Binder, who spent his vacation in nearby Lenox. A friendship began to develop and in the years to follow I was invited several times to speak at the New York Jewish Music Forum, which was founded and led by Mr. Binder.

I could not begin to talk about Binder, the musician, before voicing my gratitude to Binder, the man, who did much to help me during my early years in America. His death was a

*This speech was given on November 23, 1971 for the "Jewish Liturgical Music Society of America" and published by the Society in 1972.

great loss to the Jewish community, and a particular loss to me
who mourned a mentor and friend.

After this personal tribute, I shall now turn to my assigned topic.

When looking over Binder's musical oeuvre, one can truly
say that the tree is in the seed. Son of a *baal tefillah*, boy soprano, later alto, in an Orthodox synagogue, Binder was exposed from his earliest years to the musical tradition of the
Synagogue which, if you allow the metaphor, became his musical mother-tongue. While he developed as a musician, he
came to understand that this heritage was a mandate destined
to shape his life as a composer. Very few Jewish composers of
stature can boast such an intimate knowledge of *nusach ha-
tefillah* and Biblical cantillation in its various applications.

When in 1922 he was appointed music director at the
Free Synagogue in New York, he was painfully aware of the
low musical status of the Reform Synagogue which still held
on to the earlier materials of its founding years. He knew then
that his was the mission to bring back into Reform worship
the best musical traditions in a purified form. But that was not
all. Besides a cantor, choir and organ had to be considered,
and with this constellation an even more difficult challenge
arose. How could basically unaccompanied material be harmonized or treated contrapuntally without losing its flavor
and particular distinction? Attempts had been made by older
composers but they could not satisfy the demands of our day.
The problem of casting ancient melodies into an acceptable
modern form occupied much of Binder's creative energy. In a
late essay, he discussed his first works and concluded, "To say
that I had all the answers in 1923 would be an error. I am not
sure whether I do today, either." ("My Ideas and Theories In
My Synagogue Compositions" in *Studies in Jewish Music: Collected Writings of A. W. Binder,* New York, 1971, p. 306). His
work, then, may be summed up as a continuing process of
clarification of musical means to find satisfactory answers to a
unique problem. Binder's contribution to the American
Synagogue is twofold: restoration of *nusach ha-tefillah* and cantillation to Reform worship, and a ceaseless search for a contemporary idiom that would not distort but enhance this
melodic material.

I would like now to sketch in broad outlines the curve of Binder's liturgical music from its beginnings to the latest works. There is an early *Veshamru* published in 1919. Not many of you may know it and I suspect that by now the piece is out of print. The young composer chose the "Magen Avot" Synagogue prayer mode in E and wrote the choral parts in a fine lace work of complementary rhythms. He did not yet use the traditional turn into the major tonality on the fourth step of the scale, but there is a section in E major and a return to E minor, although not in the opening mode. The piece has some crude chordal moments in the middle, and, as a whole, is not stabilized stylistically. Yet there is a distinctive quality in the first pages, a promise that was to be fulfilled later on.

Binder's first complete service, *Hibbat Shabbat*, was published in 1928. The composer was still groping for an elusive style that would not yield to the first attack. *Hibbat Shabbat* shows imaginative modulations but is—aside from its stylistic incoherence—no more than a random collection of separate pieces following the Sabbath eve liturgy.

The breakthrough came in 1935 with the next complete service *Rinnat Shabbat*. The organ prelude, in the contrapuntal manner of Bach, takes its *cantus firmus* from the cantillation of "Shir Ha-shirim" (Song of Songs). This leads directly into the opening Psalm 92 which is based on the same material. There is unity of style, a new sense of musical texture, throughout the work, and an emphasis on the symbolic meanings of Biblical cantillation and Synagogue prayer modes: "Shir Ha-shirim" signifying Israel's love for the Sabbath, "Magen Avot," conspicuous in *Veshamru*, expressing Sabbath peace, and "Adonai Malakh" in its proud major key showing Israel as God's chosen people. As far as the harmonic language is concerned, the composer stated in the preface with fine humility, "Those of us who know only the harmonies of the latter part of the 19th century will indeed find my harmonic scheme somewhat strange. Of those I ask open-mindedness, patience and tolerance." *Rinnat Shabbat* was a bold step in Binder's career as a composer, but he was not satisfied to stop at this first achievement.

Kabbalat Shabbat followed in 1940, in answer to the need for new music called for by the revision of the Union Prayerbook. Building on his gains in the preceding *Rinnat Shabbat*, Binder enlarged his style with new elements. There is a sprightly "*Yismechu*" in true madrigal style and, as demonstrated in "Adonai Malakh," a trend which was to become a trademark of Binder's approach to *nussach* and cantillation: the declamatory unison chanting for choir, of rhythmically difficult phrases in free meters. A monumental, antique effect can be achieved by faultless precision of execution. Psalm 95, "Lekhu neranenah," is subtly conceived by breaking the opening theme with eighth rests so that the effect of breathless excitement is created.

Lekhu/lekhu/lekhu neranenah
Oh come/oh come/oh come and let us sing.

The service offers two versions of the "Kiddush," one after Lewandowski, the other freely using cantillation modes of the Pentateuch. My preference goes to the latter which, unfortunately, has little chance to replace the well entrenched Lewandowski setting.

The *Friday Eve Torah Service* which appeared for the first time in the revised Union Prayerbook is textually a checkered quilt of unrelated quotations stitched together by the rabbis of the Central Conference. Binder was obviously uncomfortable with the text and resorted to disparate material: "haftarah" cantillation, "z'mirah", Israeli song, "nusach" and a hint of "Hatikvah."

After having produced three services for Shabbat, Binder's aim was now to provide music for the entire liturgical year. The music for the High Holidays occupied him until the last years of his life. *Evening Service for the New Year,* published in 1940, was brought out later again in one volume with the *Kol Nidre* Service. It is most informative for the musician to compare the Rosh Hashanah Eve service of 1940 with the 1966 edition. Although it is basically the same music, the improving hand of the composer, wanting to bring certain details into sharper focus, is visible throughout the book.

Morning Service for the New Year of 1951 is a successful example of *Gebrauchsmusik* on a high musical level. This is best demonstrated in the opening "Hariu Ladonai," but there are also ambitious, festive pieces, such as the "Kedushah" and the "Shofar Service." I should also mention that Binder in-

cluded a melody by Isaac Offenbach, the father of Jacques
Offenbach. Isaac Offenbach was a *chazzan* in Cologne, Germany, and a prolific composer of Synagogue music. Mr. Binder had access to his manuscript material which is now in the
library of the Hebrew Union College in Cincinnati, and he in-
cluded Offenbach's *M'chalkel Chayim* for which he wrote an
organ accompaniment. In Binder's recently published essays
on Jewish music there is a study on Isaac Offenbach's life and
work. I recommend it to your attention for its historical
background and for the musical evaluation of a man whose
not so modest accomplishments were overshadowed by the
fame of his son, Jacques. ("Isaac Offenbach: His Life, Work
and Manuscript Collection" in *Studies in Jewish Music: Collected
Writings of A. W. Binder*, New York, 1971, pp. 289-303).

Arvit L'Rosh Hashanah V'Yom Kippur (1966), *Afternoon Service for the Day of Yom Kippur* (1956) and the *Neilah Service*
(1958) show a reduction of musical complexities to meet the
demands for practical usefulness. We are still dealing with
first rate melodic material, mostly culled from tradition but
the working out has become simpler. Let me point out some
details which made a particular impression on me: the
"stiffnecked" canon on the words *'Sh'eyn anu azey fanim uk'shey
oref'*, the sinister harmonic color in the "B'rosh Hashanah" section of "U'nethanneh Tokef" ('on the New Year it will be written, on Yom Kippur it will be sealed: who shall live and who
shall die'); a hint of "Artsa Alinu," a song of the early Palestinian pioneers, appropriately used for "Hayom t'amtseynu"
('Today make us strong'); the non-military, transfigured
trumpet signals for the King of Glory, in "Lift up your
heads," and finally the exquisite page of music at the end of
the *Ne'ilah* Service—*"Adonai hu ha-elohim"* ('The Lord, he is
God').

The *Three Festival Music Liturgy (Shalosh Regalim)* published in 1962, is a late work aiming at practicality, yet showing the way how to use a reduced vocabulary with distinction
and originality. The last page of *"Shiviti"* is probably the composer's most poetic utterance. The piece, belonging to the
Memorial Service, starts with a finely wrought choral section
followed by unison phrases which are supported by long held
chords. On the words "He will not forsake my soul to the

netherworld, and not allow His pious ones to see destruction," we hear no more than a childlike sing-song inflection in the voices over subtly changing chords, yet I have the compelling vision of a fainting soul sinking deeper and deeper into the pillow of eternal rest.

The last work I have chosen, *Sabbath for Israel* (Shabbat L'Yisrael) published in 1954, occupies a unique position in Binder's output. In the twenties, Binder began to collect Israeli—at that time, Palestinian—folksongs and published them as solo pieces with simple piano accompaniments. Later, in 1942, he came forth with a set of choral arrangements of exemplary quality, such as *Kacha-Kach.*

On his visits to Israel, Binder tried to establish closer contact between Israeli and Jewish-American composers. The musical outcome of this endeavor is the Sabbath Eve Service, *Sabbath for Israel.* It is Binder's most artful, most complex and, in matters of form, his most expansive work among his liturgical compositions, showing a blend of the Ashkenazic tradition with the emerging style of Israeli music. Although Binder does not use actual Israeli tunes, he creates a striking similarity as in "Lekhah Dodi" which I rate as the composer's most charming, probably even his most perfect liturgical piece. "Mi Khamokha," hinting at Miriam's dance, described in the book of Exodus, is cast into the form of a *hora; "Yismechu"* excels in contrapuntal finesse; *"Adon Olam,"* for the first time in Binder's various settings of the text, appears as a hymn, thus fulfilling its true liturgical purpose. The tune, of Sephardic lineage, is treated ingeniously in a different manner from verse to verse, and finally crowned with a canon preceding a short coda.

The bringing together of East and West, as exemplified on a large scale in this work, may be observed in miniature size in the piano variations on a Yemenite theme. In variation No. 6 the Oriental theme is twice interrupted by a recitative which, using the same notes as the theme, manages to change it into an Ashkenazic chant, thus emphasizing the unity of *K'lal Yisrael.*

Mr. Binder must have been disappointed that his efforts to create a close bond between Israeli and American-Jewish composers did not come to fruition. The Israeli composers still look upon Jewish music of other countries as *galut* music and are reluctant to accept it. This may change in years to come. The growing pains of a young country may be the reason for so adolescent an attitude. For the time being, Binder's *Sabbath for Israel* is still a lonely work waiting to be discovered by those who inspired it.

But this could in no way impair Binder's commanding position as a Jewish musician in America. His activities as composer, author, lecturer, teacher and organizer had an enormous influence on all aspects of Jewish music, extending even to the field of hymnology. As musical editor of the Union Hymnal of 1932, he tried to channel congregational singing into more acceptable ways than in the early days of Reform Judaism. We must say, in all honesty, that his aim was not fully achieved. But, having been involved myself in a similar project, I am in sympathy with a composer whose artistic strivings—as in my case—were, most likely, frustrated by a committee of half-and non-musicians who, as the book of Jonah has it, cannot discern between their right hand and their left hand.

And now, as a concluding question, what shall we say about the future of Binder's musical bequest to the Synagogue at a time when jazz, rock and electronic devices are making inroads into the music of the Synagogue? I cannot speak for Mr. Binder and tell you what his reaction might have been.

Let me, instead, quote a Talmudic statement: "Whosoever intones the Holy Scriptures in the manner of secular song offends the Torah." This may well be applied to our prayers which, for that matter, come in many instances from the Torah itself. We are not prepared to say how long the new trend will last but of one thing we may be sure—true values will not easily be wiped out by the corrosion of time. Let us remember the inscription on Mr. Binder's tombstone, *Ha-manginah nisheret*, the melody remains. And *manginah* means for me not just any melody, but that melody alone which springs from a people's historic experience.

HUGO CHAIM ADLER*
(1894-1955)

My first meeting with Hugo Chaim Adler took place in Germany when I traveled from Frankfurt to Mannheim in September 1936 to seek out this man whose music had caught my interest. We had a lively afternoon of music making and conversation, and as I left he presented me with his latest work, the score of *Shirah Chadashah*, a large collection of pieces for the Synagogue.

Hugo's son Hans, at that time a small boy, escorted me to the trolley to make sure that I took the right line for the railroad station. This Hans, now called Samuel, is today Chairman of the Composition Department at the Eastman School of Music in Rochester, N.Y., and has become a much performed and well-known composer, thus continuing the line of distinguished composers who were sons of cantors: Jacques Offenbach, Kurt Weill, Paul Dessau, Hugo Weisgall.

In 1936 we were living under the oppression of the Hitler regime and thoughts of emigration were uppermost in our minds. I came to America in 1937. On leaving my first position in Buffalo, I settled in Boston in 1941 to assume duties as music director and organist of Temple Israel. When I discovered that Hugo Chaim Adler had been appointed cantor at Temple Emanuael in nearby Worcester, the thread of our acquaintance was taken up again.

A genuine friendship developed and we met almost regularly in intervals of four to six weeks. There was a vivid exchange of compositions, of ideas, planning of programs,

*This article appeared in *Jewish Music Notes*, Fall Issue of 1956. The passage about Samuel H. Adler has been added.

113

speculation on the future of Synagogue music, and critical analysis. The warm atmosphere of the Adler home, their family life, meals, observance of holidays—all created a bond of affection far beyond the interests of our professional lives.

Cantor Adler was a scholarly man and widely read in many fields of Jewish knowledge. He possessed that fine simplicity of learning which courses freely through the narrow channels of everyday living. Things went well for Hugo and his family and they were happy in their newly established life. Then, in 1948, a supreme crisis set in. Sickness struck Hugo and the amputation of one leg became necessary. The man who used to fret under the discomforts of a cold turned into a model of heroism. No complaints, no bitterness. He endured the trial, came back from the hospital (where the Book of Job had comforted him) composed new music, rehearsed the choir, sang at services, taught and prepared his favorite project, the Annual Jewish Music Festival of Temple Emanuel, Worcester. My love and admiration for the man were now mingled with awe for the nobility of a spirit whose dedication could not be deflected from its course, even under the stress of severe misfortune.

Seven years later the dreadful disease recurred. He battled with courage and determination, but to no avail. When I visited him at his sickbed in a Boston hospital he said with a tired voice: "I am auditioning for the Choir of the Cherubim."

Months of intense suffering followed. I saw him every other week in Worcester, and each time he had faded noticeably. In the last weeks of his life his interest in mundane matters vanished almost completely: his mind was turned to another life. Speech became harder and harder but he listened and was still attentive to problems of musical composition. It was in one of our last conversations that he said with the humility characteristic of the man and the musician: "I have not learned enough."

We buried him on December 26, 1955. When we put our shoulders to the casket as pall bearers we carried a light body, diminished by physical suffering, but also the weight of visitation, pain and magnificent endurance.

Hugo Chaim Adler left a large number of musical works, some published but most of them still in manuscript. There are the early oratorios and cantatas, "Job" (words, in free rendition of the Bible, by Max Gruenwald), "An Zion" (text by Yehuda Halevi, in German translation by Franz Rosenzweig), "Balak and Bileam," later revised, and *"Akedah,"* a biblical legend based on Genesis, Chapter 22 and passages from *Mishnah* and *Aggadah.*

Among the large scale works written in America are "Jonah" (biblical text), "Behold the Jew" (words by Ada Jackson), "Bearers of Light" (new version of an older work), which is a Chanukkah Cantata with words by Max Gruenwald, in English translation by Alexander Schindler.

In his last year Hugo often discussed his plan to revise *"Akedah,"* composed in 1938. The text is of the most profound beauty, and the work was always especially close to the composer's heart. The music with its choruses, recitatives, arias, and duets reflects Hugo's unending love for the art of Johann Sebastian Bach.

Then there are the innumerable works for the Synagogue: The monumental collection *Shirah Chadashah*, "Music for the Synagogue" (prize winning work for a contest sponsored by the Central Conference of American Rabbis), *Avodat Habonim* a children's Service, *Nachlat Yisrael*, a Friday Eve Service according to the Union Prayer Book, *Pirchey Shabbat*, a collection of twelve lesser known *Zemirot* of the German tradition in settings for choir and organ, a Sabbath Service for solo voice and organ, and many individual pieces, anthems and arrangements of folksongs. One of his last labors was the recasting of Lewandowski's music for use in the American Reform Synagogue.

The Annual Jewish Music Festival of Temple Emanuel, Worcester, which Hugo founded and guided through fifteen seasons, saw the first performances of some of his major works, such as "Behold the Jew," "Jonah," the new version of "Balak and Balaam" and "Bearers of Light," but also the rearranging of music by old masters. Thus we have Adler's versions of Carissimi's "Judgment of Solomon," of Mozart's youthful oratorio "Judith" and Marcello's "Nineteenth Psalm," an ingratiating elaboration in cantata form with chorus, recitative, aria and an instrumental interlude derived from one of Marcello's trio sonatas.

Huge Chaim Adler's output was mostly in the forms of vocal music. His instrumental works, known to me, are an early and difficult toccata for organ, a trio for two violins and piano ("The Jewish Year in Melody"), a set of "Three Pieces" for violin and piano (*Tsarah*—Affliction, *Redifah*—Persecution, and *Akedah*—Sacrifice) and "Six Small Preludes" for organ.

The style of Adler's music in his early works was a groping, dissonant chromaticism, in keeping with the general trend after the First World War, particularly under the influence of his teacher Ernest Toch who at that time was one of the leaders among young composers in Germany. There was energy, expansion and magnitude in these first works but the blemishes of a transitory stage cannot be overlooked.

Later on Adler's means of musical expression became much more conservative. A specialist in choral music, he acquired the skill to write a moderately contemporary, yet distinctive, polyphony, challenging to professional groups but also accessible to amateur choirs. His unique gift was a clear and singable melody but as a harmonist he was not always so sure. Yet, his concluding cadences come sometimes like sudden and compelling revelations.

In some of his smaller anthems he managed a perfect blending of all elements. I am thinking of pieces like *Shomer Yisrael, Haneros Halolu,* "Early will I seek Thee," "By the Waters of Babylon," which have become part of the repertoire of many Synagogues and will stay alive for a long time to come. It is music beautifully achieved, and touched by the quality of a man who was called to his work by earnestness of faith and by the unquestioning loyalty to his heritage.

HEINRICH SCHALIT*
(1886-1976)

*... Dieser erst oben
biegt sich zur Leier*
Only this one above
bends into a lyre.

Thus, Rilke in the seventeenth of his "Sonnets to Orpheus." Obscure lines when taken out of context. As the concluding verses of the complete poem, they tell us that many branches of the family tree are coarse, or will break but that the last one may bend into the shape of a lyre—poetry or music.

It was music with Salomone Rossi (1570-1630), scion of an illustrious Jewish family in Mantua, and it was music again in the case of Heinrich Schalit, descendant of a Viennese Jewish family that began to distinguish itself in the second half of the 19th century. The father, Joseph Schalit, was an acknowledged Hebraist. Heinrich's brothers worked in other fields: the oldest, Isidor, was co-worker, friend and sometimes secretary of Theodor Herzl; Leon, writer and anglicist, was the translator into German of the works of Galsworthy, one of the most widely read authors of the period.

Heinrich Schalit's musical education leads us back into the history of music. He studied with the composer Robert Fuchs (1847-1927) who was considered one of the greatest teachers of composition in his time. His works are hardly played anymore but—irony of ironies—a joke about him has not yet lost its currency. Joseph Hellmesberger (1855-1907), conductor,

*This article appeared in the *Journal of Synagogue Music*, June 1976. By necessity, some parts are repeated from the essay "The Influence of German-Jewish Composers on the American Synagogue."

violinist, and much quoted wit, after hearing a work by Fuchs, said *"Fuchs, das hast du ganz gestohlen"* (Fox, this you have stolen entirely), a pun on the first line of a well-known German children's song *"Fuchs, du hast die Gans gestohlen"* (Fox, you have stolen the goose).

Another teacher of Schalit's was Joseph Labor (1842-1924), a blind pianist, organist and composer who, according to Schalit's account, must have been an extraordinary musician. Labor himself had studied with Simon Sechter (1788-1867), famous theorist in the history of music, who wrote three volumes *Die Grundsätze der musikalischen Komposition, The Foundations of Musical Composition.* It is known that Franz Schubert in the last year of his life, after having created a vast library of masterworks, considered studying with Sechter to improve his counterpoint. Through Schubert's early death (November 19, 1828) the plan came to nothing. Anton Bruckner (1824-1896) however was a full-time student of Sechter, faithfully following his teacher's insistence on regular exercises in all branches of counterpoint.

Robert Fuchs and Josef Labor—the latter, incidentally, also a teacher of Arnold Schönberg—saw to it that Schalit's talent got a solid grounding in technical competence. His early works, all secular, show him second to none in compositional technique. I have before me op. 17 *Sechs Liebeslieder* (Six Love Songs), published by Universal Edition, one of the most reputable houses in Europe. These songs are based on poems by Max Dauthendey (1867-1918), "rhapsodist of blessed abundance," as Richard Dehmel called him. The poems are sensuous throughout, but not marred by the vulgarity that is so much in evidence in contemporary poetry. There is no doubt where Dauthendey belongs in the history of literature: He is a true child of a period we called *"Jugendstil"* a mixture of medievalism, folksong simplicity and over-bred, self-indulgent sensibility. However, I will not minimize the quality of verses such as:

> *Deine Augen sind himmlische Brücken,*
> *Wie nach dem Regen im Bogen*
> *Sieben Freuden am Himmel einzogen,*
> *So können deine Augen beglücken.*

(Your eyes are heavenly bridges,
as after the rain in a bow
seven joys appear in the skies—
thus your eyes bring bliss to me).

Schalit's music is the work of a master in musical form as well
as in the sweeping fullness and independence of the accompaniment. Early in his life, like Mahler, Schalit broke with the
then fashionable style of Hugo Wolf with its declamatory
treatment of the voice which had to depend on the accompaniment to make any sense at all. In his Love Songs Schalit
created singable melodies, not mere fragments, that were
complete in themselves.

As a young man of twenty, Schalit moved to Munich to
take up a teaching career. Among his students were the
daughter of the piano builder Steinway, and one of the
daughers of Samuel Clemens (Mark Twain). I remember that
when I was a student of the State Academy of Music in
Munich, Schalit's name was already known to me as composer
and pianist. (He had been a pupil of Leschetitzky in piano).
But I met him for the first time in Rochester, New York; then
more often in Providence, Rhode Island, where he served as
organist at the Reform Temple. After a short period as organist in Hollywood, California, he retired to Denver, Col-
orado. Later he built a mountain cottage in Evergreen, near
Denver, where I visited him and his wife Hilda, on several occasions. He was amused when I called him "my ever green
composer." In our personal relationship Schalit was always
friendly and cordial and spoke well of my work. Basically, he
was not a socially minded person and preferred to stay by
himself. Producing music, especially in his later years, was a
slow, often painful process—partly due to his failing
eyesight—and he never stopped revising his works.

But I am ahead of myself. Returning to Munich it is important to relate that in 1927 he was appointed organist of the
Synagogue, and in this position he was exposed to the music of
Emanuel Kirschner, the Synagogue's cantor-composer who was
a conservative follower of Lewandowski. Challenged to seek
new ways, Schalit gave up an already recognized career in the
field of secular music which had begun auspiciously at the age

of twenty when he won the Austrian State Prize in Composition with a piano quartet.

It must have been around 1930 that Schalit turned to Jewish liturgical music. His first piece, as he once told me, was the *V'shamru*, now part of his Friday Eve Service. It is a fullblown masterpiece and I can well imagine that at that time Schalit came to a decision that was to determine his future career as a composer. Continuing in the secular field, he would have been one among other good composers. In the liturgical field he offered something entirely new, a musical approach that would influence the style of Jewish liturgical music. I am not thinking here of practical considerations. Writing liturgical music became for Schalit a sacred calling to the almost complete exclusion of any other musical forms. His basic achievement, called *Eine Freitag Abend Liturgie*, appeared in Germany in 1933 and was revised and newly published in America in 1951, under the title *Liturgiah shel Leyl Sabbat*. I have the first German edition of the work, published by the composer himself. This is not the place to go into a detailed comparison between the German and American editions, although there are striking differences worth exploring. The most important addition to the American publication is the inclusion of Psalm 98 in the *Kabbalat Shabbat* section. It is an extensive composition bearing the dedication "To the Genius and Humanitarian Albert Einstein." This dedication is by no means presumptuous. I consider this Psalm as Schalit's most perfect, his most ambitious liturgical work.

Trying to understand Schalit's aims as a composer of Synagogue music, I shall translate some of his illuminating sentences from the German preface of the first edition:

"It is an obligation for the creative minds among Jewish musicians to prepare a change in style and outlook, to create a new, unified liturgical music growing out of the soil of the old-new, significant and valuable source material offered by Idelsohn. The unorganic mixture of traditional cantorial chants with congregational and choral music in the German style of the 19th century must be eliminated." And further: "This work is trying to fulfill the demands which must be made today for the rejuvenation of our Temple music. Its style is rooted in the timelessness of old Hebrew motifs for

Bible and Prayer, motifs which form the germinal cells for the
musical substance of this work. Also the freely invented parts
rest on the foundation of Hebrew-Oriental melody."

Thus, Schalit was the first composer to grasp the importance of the material offered by Avraham Zvi Idelsohn in his
collection of Oriental-Jewish chants. Schalit's preference is
clear but he did not neglect the Ashkenazic tradition either, as
shown in his settings of *L'chu n'rannenah, Adonai malach* and
Vay'chulu. In the preface to the American edition, Schalit
speaks of "our ancestral memory," and I see it at work when,
without folkloristic models, the composer must rely on the infallibility of that memory. For all this melodic material Schalit
avoided the harmonic idiom of the 19th century, as
exemplified by Lewandowski. He forged his own language, a
tart diatonicism which he treats in contrapuntal fashion, as in
L'cha Dodi, or in homophonic textures, tellingly dissonant, as
in *Tov l'hodot.*

On the 1st of December 1975 I gave a lecture at the
"Conference on the Music of the American Synagogue," at the
School of Sacred Music in New York, which is a branch of the
Hebrew Union College. I wrote the lecture ahead of time and
sent a copy to Schalit. He answered on September 27, 1975,
some three months before his 90th birthday. It was to be his
last letter to me and I shall quote what is pertinent to our topic: "I read your interesting essay and I cannot tell you how
deeply I appreciate your remarks about my music and myself.
I know that you were one of the first who recognized the new
style. May I tell you in brief the story of the *Freitag Abend
Liturgie:* In early spring of 1931 when I returned to Munich
from a visit in Rochester, New York, I was already a well-
know composer in Germany, especially in Munich, Augsburg,
Frankfurt, Dresden, Berlin, etc. probably because of the performance of my Hymn *"In Ewigkeit".* It was then that the capable choir director of the Leo Baeck Synagogue in Berlin, who
had at his disposal a choir of over 30 singers as well as a fine
organ, approached me to write a new Service. Many people
didn't like the German style of Lewandowski anymore, and
there was a vacuum in Synagogue music. Weinbaum (the choir
director) came from Berlin to Landeck (Tyrol), presumably on
a vacation trip in the sumer of 1931, to talk it over with me. I

was enraptured by the idea and promised to compose a Service according to the Berlin prayerbook. In the fall of 1931 I composed the Service within 6 weeks and it was sung in the Temple in the fall of 1932 with young Janowsky at the organ. The reaction was divided. Some liked it very much, among them Arno Nadel, Alfred Einstein, and Curt Sachs. Other people rejected it. After several repetitions they said to Rabbi Baeck 'If this is to be our future Synagogue music, we'll leave the Temple.' Well, they didn't have to leave because the Nazis in 1933 took good care of their not coming anymore. One of the critics said to me 'It will take at least 30 years until people will understand and accept your music.' I didn't believe it but now I do. It was a most beautiful performance and I was proud at the age of 46. But now, being almost 90, I am humble and think that our younger generation should carry on. Again, many thanks for your fine article, I hope they will appreciate it in New York too."

I have dwelt on the Friday Eve Service at such length because it marked a turning point in the composer's life. It may be well to remember that Schalit's name is more than a mere coincidence. We pronounce it Schalit (stress on the first syllable), but as a Hebrew word, Schalit (stress on the second syllable) means Leader, Master. Could there be a better name for a man who initiated a stylistic change in Western Synagogue music and became a master of his craft?

Much important music came from his pen in later years: A capella pieces, a Shabbat Morning Service, another Friday Eve Service, on a smaller scale, song cycles, cantatas based on Israeli folk music, anthems, etc. But I think of his *Liturgiah shel Leyl Shabbat* as his most enduring work, coloring all that was yet to come. Schalit's favorite words for sacred, not necessarily liturgical, texts were taken from the Hebrew poets of 11th century Spain: Yehuda Halevi and Ibn Gabirol. Shortly before his death (February 3, 1976) he wrote his last composition, based on words by Ibn Gabirol. The music shows that noble simplicity of statement, the wisdom, which is the result of a life-long search for perfection. The text begins with the words: "Forget thine affliction," and ends with "sunlight shall glow with a sevenfold ray." Here is the rainbow again, as in No. 4 of the "Liebeslieder." But now it has become something else. Not the seven earthly joys of the Dauthendey poem but the radiance of a never setting sun.

Postscript

The first edition of Schalit's Friday Eve Service was not engraved but lithographed after the script of a Munich copyist. I immediately recognized it as the hand of the copyist who had also worked for me. My thoughts took a sudden turn to the Purim song *Shoshannat Yaakov*, Lily of Jacob. After blessings for Mordechai and Esther, the song ends: "*V'gam Charvono zachur l'tov.*" "And also Charvono shall be remembered for good." He was the scribe who on a night when King Ahasverus couldn't sleep, read the Chronicles of the Land with the passage telling of Mordechai's merits for the King's welfare. This led to Haman's downfall and to the salvation of the Jewish people.

Following the example of the Purim song, the Munich scribe should now find a place at the end of this essay. His name was Boehm.

NINE REVIEWS

VINAVER'S ANTHOLOGY*

This new *Anthology of Jewish Music* (E.B. Marks, New York, 1955)—if its subtitle "Sacred Chant and Religious Folk Song of the Eastern European Jews" is to be taken seriously—is not quite consistent in its aims, because the book also includes works by Frederick Jacobi and Arnold Schönberg. The first part of the volume concerns itself with "Sacred Chant," the term "Chant" being interpreted to mean actual chant as well as choral settings. The second part offers "Religious Folk Song."

The value of the book rests on the editor's notation of unaccompanied recitatives. Pieces such as *Mosay Timloch* (page 78) with its expressive interpretation of the text, Psalm 130 (page 201) in its straightforward dignity, *Kol M'kadeysh Sh'vii* (page 226) using pliable variations of the mode for a close fitting of words and music, should be mentioned here. Our prize goes to *Ashrey Hoom*, from the *Rosh Hashonoh* Service, a *chassidic* chant as sung by the *Baal T'fillah* at the Rabbi's court in Skiernowice, Poland. It is a modal theme with three variations, highly imaginative, and an outstanding example of a self-reliant melodic art.

Cut down to its good recitative material the book would have sufficed, and brought forth our unmixed gratitude for the editor's first-hand notations. We would then have had a small volume only, but the loss of weight would have been compensated for by a gain in stature.

What shall we say about the pages and pages of interminable choral music where the fantastic, freely roaming recitative stands in juxtaposition with embarrassingly timid choral

*This review appeared in the *Menorah Journal*, Spring-Summer issue, 1956.

passages? When the composers in this anthology—masters of the recitative, to be sure—write harmonized choral music a strange transformation takes place: they become stiff, uncomfortable, hunchbacked as it were. (Exceptions and half-exceptions will be discussed later). This holds true even if we admit that there are marked differences of talent and skill. The fluent music of Alman, for instance, is far superior to the music of A. M. Bernstein or Minkowski. The latter's long composition *Ato Noseyn Yod*, published here for the first time, excels in fine recitative work and all but suffocates under a dead weight of harmonic commonplaces. In this type of music one is relieved when an occasional unison choral phrase restores the uncluttered beauty of a melodic turn.

Our point can be brought home most sharply in the case of Moses Milner. His ambitious *Un'saneh Tokef* from the *Rosh Hashonoh* Service is a much overrated work. It is sad to see a composer, who achieved in a song such as *In Cheder* a triumph of folk consciousness within the scope of his musical resources, come to grief when faced with the task of an extended choral work. His technique not being equal to such demands, he must rely on the crumbs picked from the table of Western music culture. The academic fugato (pages 107-108) is beneath any serious discussion; but then, all of a sudden, the bottom line on page 108 and the closing cadences on page 113 reveal what Milner could have become with a stronger musical intellect to guide his undoubted talent.

The old-time Jewish composer, on leaving his home ground of the unaccompanied recitative, was at a loss as soon as he began to apply the means of harmony and counterpoint to the melodic material of his own heritage. We understand the difficulties of such first attempts, but in recent decades much progress has been made. The free techniques of contemporary music have opened up possibilities undreamed of by the older generation. Mr. Vinaver's Anthology is flagrantly amiss in not representing some of the composers (Frederick Jacobi excepted) who have without any doubt narrowed the gap between Jewish melody and Western art forms: Adler, Bloch, Binder, Chajes, Freed, Helfman, Saminsky, Schalit, Weiner, Weinberg and others. The reproach holds even if this anthology is only the first in a series to follow.

After all, the present anthology supposedly covers the ground from the earliest Biblical chant up to Schönberg. The contemporary works Mr. Vinaver offers are eight numbers of his own composition, two pieces by the Swedish cantor Leo Rosenblueth, one work each by Frederick Jacobi, Erich Itor Kahn and Arnold Schönberg. The works by Vinaver and Rosenblueth stand in the middle between the old and new.

Rosenblueth has a decided flair for composition and writes some excellent music (such as the opening pages of the *Kedushah*), but he lacks the strength to sustain the level. His music shows imagination; the steady criss-cross of styles, however, betrays a musical mind not strong enough to control all details of a musical composition from a firmly established stylistic center.

Mr. Vinaver's works have similar tendencies. There is a striving for sound effects, half-hearted attempts at modernism, and a lack of coherence in matters of style. While the melodic material is fine throughout, the creative spark is not hot enough to melt all the elements into a pure-sounding alloy. His best efforts seem to us Psalms 24 and 126, although the unidiomatic seventh and ninth chords spoil much of the Hebraic flavor the composer is striving for. Page 197 (the work is Psalm 126) points a path that could be pursued to good advantage.

Far and away the outstanding modern work of the collection is Frederick Jacobi's *Teyfen L'hakshiv*, after a text by Saadia Gaon. Published in 1942 by the Bloch Company, it appears here in a reprint. Among Jacobi's works for the Synagogue this composition ranks with his best. There is an uncompromising starkness of texture, a compelling accord between melodic turn and harmonic idiom, and an admirable concentration that allows no lapses into foreign media of expression.

Erich Itor Kahn's madrigal treatment of *chassidic* dance melodies, published here for the first time, is enormously skillful but remains a questionable experiment. Such melodies, it seems to us, seek a different kind of fulfilment in art music.

Arnold Schönberg's composition of Psalm 130 was written especially for this anthology. It is conceived for six-part *a capella* chorus, partly sung, partly spoken in fixed rhythm.

The work is a delicate maze of the most subtle, unsingable chromatic counterpoint. One stands in awe before this piece of paper-music that seems destined to remain buried within the pages of this expensive anthology as in a satin-lined coffin.

The second part of the *anthology* is filled with religious folk songs, many of them again in first-hand notation by the editor. (We were surprised to find on page 234 *Yom Zeh L'Yisroeyl* marked as a first-hand notation. The same melody is to be found elsewhere too, e.g. in the music supplement of the Sabbath book by Abraham E. Millgram). With the exception of two choral numbers everything in this section comes as unaccompanied melody.

There is some fine material but also a lot of mediocre tunes, especially in the chapter of *Chassidic Niggunim* with their ever-recurring clichés so well known through other collections. This *doi-doi-bam-bam* music obviously can only come to life by the exalted rendition of the true *chassid;* but we submit that a song by Schubert or an aria by Handel has intrinsic musical value, quite apart from the aspect of inspired or uninspired performance. The intrinsic musical value of these *Niggunim* is small indeed—a painful thing to say when one considers the tremendous effect this music has had within the *chassidic* movement.

The claims Mr. Vinaver makes in the preface to his *Anthology* are so sweeping that a sense of disappointment cannot be avoided when studying a work which is full of material, or rather types of material, available also in other collections, notably the works of A. Z. Idelsohn and Gershon Ephros. In reading the preface one may be misled into thinking that in the field of Jewish music compilation, very little happened B.C.—that is, Before Chemjo.

The layout and printing of the book are beautiful; but misprints of music notations abound. All texts are given in Hebrew and English. Short, instructive commentaries precede each number. A fine drawing by Marc Chagall serves as frontispiece: it shows King David with crown and harp, and in the background a Jewish fiddler of the ghetto—a late descendant of the royal singer. Although this particular *klezmer* uses the left hand for his bow, he may well have been the founder of a new royal line of magnificent violinists. We mean the Heifetzes, Milsteins and Sterns.

AVODAT SHABBAT*

A Friday Evening Service by Herman Berlinski.
Mercury Music Corporation

Here is a Service which by its scope and seriousness stands out among contemporary works for the Synagogue. We pay our respects to a composer who defies common usefulness and prefers to go his own way in a personal interpretation of traditional prayer texts.

The very ambition which animates the pages of this Service is also its danger. There is a predilection for involved harmony and an obsession with heavy textures, rarely allowing for clear, unequivocal statements. Although there are passages in a purely diatonic style, the prevalence of chromatic harmony indicates the composer's natural leaning.

For specific remarks let us consider some individual pieces. *L'cho Dodi* is based on a simple Sephardic melody in F, comprising no more than six notes in range, and avoiding the leading note. This might well be harmonized in the mixolydian mode; but in the very exposition of the theme, pronounced by the cantor, Berlinski creates doubts by mixing E flats with E naturals, A flats with A naturals. This opening statement is followed immediately by a choral setting of the same tune, now in strictly diatonic F major harmony—a stylistic vacillation more often encountered in the course of the work.

Tov L'hodos starts with a splendid theme recurring throughout the piece in rondo fashion. Some of the intervening episodes are disturbing, especially where picturesque ef-

*This review appeared in *The Cantor's Voice*, December 1961.

131

fects are attempted, as in the harp accompaniment to the
words *alei higoyon bechinor.*

Sh'ma and *Veohavto* make use of Solomon Rosowsky's research in biblical cantillation. Unfortunately, the fine melodic
material is smothered under a heavy organ accompaniment.

Veohavto presents a special problem. Each line of the Hebrew text, sung by the cantor, is followed by an *a capella* choral
setting of the corresponding English words. This situation,
which perhaps should never have been brought about, may be
altogether beyond a satisfactory solution. There is no musical
integration between the Hebrew and English sections, with the
exception of the very last line. Here the choral passage rests
on octaves and closes with a simple cadence, lightly harmonized and related melodically to the preceding cantillation.

Mi Chomocho, after a festive, richly textured opening, is a
promising piece that deteriorates into private musings *(noro
s'hilos ose fele)* not easily justified by the text, and most certainly not by the musical impulse of the beginning which is
stunted before given a chance to develop its full potential.

Hashkiveynu, to this reviewer's taste, is an overwrought
piece. A passionate text, such as this, would gain by a steady
frame-like musical treatment.

Adon Olom, built on a good sturdy tune, is skillfully man-
ipulated to sound like a strophic hymn without actually being
composed as such. Each second line of the two line stanzas is
the same, while the preceding first lines differ in subtle ways,
yet give the illusion of strophic similarity. This device, to the
detriment of the piece, is broken in the fourth stanza. Here
the composer reaches for a climax by leading the soprano in
slowly rising chromatic steps from middle G to high A flat.

Taken as a whole, the work is taxing in its vocal demands
and requires a well trained chorus, preferably with professional lead voices. The organ writing, often effective, suffers
at times from pianistic doublings which contradict the nature
of the instruemnt.

It need not be emphasized that a composer of Berlinski's
standing writes a highly professional score, and that *Avodat
shabbat* is a contribution to be reckoned with in the fast growing literature of new Synagogue music.

FIVE PRELUDES*

(From the Sacred Service for the Sabbath Eve, Op. 122)
by Mario Castelnuovo-Tedesco, Leeds Music Corporation

New organ music for the Synagogue will be eagerly seized upon by every temple organist who is tired of forever playing the established organ repertoire of the church. The last few decades have witnessed a renewal of vocal music for the Synagogue and a modern liturgical style is clearly discernible. One should expect contemporary Jewish composers to parallel this development with music for organ. However, little has been done so far and it is disappointing to see that Castelnuovo-Tedesco's Five Preludes do not add weight to the literature of organ music for Jewish worship.

Castelnuovo-Tedesco thinks in short motives which he develops in facile sequences, canons and tonal transpositions. His harmonic language is the fading romantic chromaticism of yesterday, spiced with impressionistic devices. "Contemplation" is a composite of three unrelated sections. "Adoration" suffers from a distinctly operatic gesture, but holds well together formally. "Invocation" seems to be the best of the five pieces. It is the only one with a Jewish flavor; the melody, strikingly enhanced by a virile rhythmic accompaniment, has a genuine declamatory character. "Silent devotion" is too pianistic in its writing for organ. "Lamentation," based on an attractive theme, calls for *vox humana* and tremulant, the "salt-and-water stops" of the organ. An additional direction "weeping" is carrying the sentiment too far.

*The following Seven Reviews appeared between 1952 and 1966 in the Jewish Welfare Board's magazine *Circle*.

There is no room in a review to go into a lengthy discussion of what organ music for the Synagogue should be. Only this: frugality of means would seem to be a desirable and honest start for an almost new branch of musical literature. Whether organ pieces for the Synagogue should be based on Hebrew themes or freely conceived (as in the case of Castelnuovo-Tedesco) each composer must decide for himself. But one thing is sure: what we require is—to say it metaphorically—straight furniture; the curved and softly padded furniture of yesterday does not answer our needs. Castelnuovo-Tedesco's Preludes belong to the latter category.

SACRED SERVICE

by Salomone Rossi
(Transcribed for the American Synagogue by Isadore
Freed, Transcontinental Music Corporation)

Isadore Freed, whose musical contributions to the American Synagogue are manifold, deserves our special gratitude for having turned his attention to the music of Salomone Rossi, a Jewish-Italian composer who flourished at the turn of the 16th century. The result is a transcribed Friday Eve Service, practical in dimensions, and mainly designed for use in Reform worship.

In this type of endeavor two roads are open: faithful adaption or the free use of old material as a basis for a modern work. Dr. Freed chose the first way and has done a remarkably fine job of re-arranging. Only a few texts of the musical responses and prayers, used in the American Reform Synagogue today, are to be found in the work which Rossi published in 1623 under the title *Hashirim Asher Lishlomo: Tov L'hodos, Borechu, Hashkivenu, Adon Olom.* Everything else had to be adapted from music written for other texts, mainly Psalms. Dr. Freed solved the problem with tact, insight and an eye for general usefulness. (Until the recent reissue by the Sacred Music Press of Naumbourg's Rossi collection of 1876, Rossi's music had been difficult of access, except for a few odd pieces in the French publisher's Salabert *Mizmor* series.)

Freed's work succeeds in lifting the veil of hearsay from Rossi's music; this half-forgotten world of Jewish Renaissance music has become a reality again, and will surely find its way into the repertoire of our synagogues. The splendid organ prelude, drawn from Rossi's composition of Psalm 80, is a valuable addition.

Rossi, court musician in Mantua, and a composer of secular fame, aimed at a reform of Jewish liturgical music by introducing harmony and counterpoint, "the rules of musical art" as he called them, to the music of the Synagogue. His position as a reformer makes him an important figure in a historical sense but only the quality of the music as such can justify a revival. The artful simplicity of Rossi's music, the purity and reticence of his harmonic progressions, are as fresh today as they were three hundred years ago. The aloof, serene beauty of this music, conceived in the finely wrought homophonic style of the late Renaissance, brings a rare quality to the music of the Synagogue which so often indulges in a blunt appeal to the more obvious emotions. We should not get too much involved in the question just how Jewish Rossi's music is. Let it be enough that it is music written by a Jew for Jewish worship.

The layout of the book with its handsomely designed cover bespeaks the publisher's interest in Dr. Freed's project.

HARMONIZING THE JEWISH MODES

By Isadore Freed, The Sacred Music Press

In the last chapter of his book *Jewish Music* (1929), A. Z. Idelsohn deals briefly and effectively with the problem of harmony, as applied to the Jewish modes. Almost thirty years later Eric Werner, in his manual "In the Choir Loft" (1957), elucidates the subject further and makes a distinct contribution by notating the modes in motivic rather than in scale form. Isadore Freed's *Harmonizing the Jewish Modes* represents the first specialized treatise as a solid base for further exploration.

It is evident that in the early and middle 19th century composers of Synagogue music were so hypnotized by the Tonic-Dominant system that they could not arrive at an idiomatic harmonization of modal melodies. Even Beethoven who wrote his *Dankgesang* (String Quartet op. 132) by his own designation "in the Lydian Mode" did not succeed in creating a firm impression of the Church Mode; we are inclined to hear the piece in C rather than in F.

Beginning with the late 19th century steady drops of new harmonic devices split the rock of Tonic-Dominant relationship; the time had come to re-evaluate the harmonic possibilities inherent in modal chants.

Dr. Freed has laid out a plan of study derived from his course at the Hebrew Union School of Sacred Music in New York. The modes, their cadences and modulations, are fully explained; there are many helpful practical suggestions and a wealth of musical examples. Everything is aimed at the common sense level of average comprehension, and this is exactly what a text book of this kind should offer. One could question

137

the wisdom of perpetuating four-part harmony as an accepted norm; three or even two-part writing might often prove to be more pliable for modal material. Also, judicious use of unison passages would have warranted a chapter of advice and example. Contrapuntal treatment, or the building of chords on a system other than thirds, clearly was not within the scope of this work and must await further studies.

The book abounds in good observations of a general nature. However, a sentence like, "In fact, great art is timeless" is not particularly engaging, and one could take issue with the condescension toward the "naivete" of 16th century harmony in a statement such as this: "Today we know our chords. We are no longer afraid of dissonances; for dissonance has been finally emancipated." A theoretical myth that the plagal cadence can be explained as a Dominant-Tonic progression, by viewing the IV chord as 7-9-11 of the Dominant, with 1-3-5 missing, is not worthy of repetition. It is like saying that a roof can stand in air with neither house nor cellar under it.

But these are minor exceptions. There can be no doubt that Dr. Freed has made a thoroughly practical contribution to a neglected field of musical harmony. His teaching is bound to bear fruit among the students who have the good fortune to be guided by a man of Dr. Freed's musical talent, intelligence and taste.

KOL RINAH B'OHALEY ISRAEL

A Sabbath Service of Israel, Mills Music Inc.

The Israeli composer who wishes to write for the Synagogue will find little encouragement in his own country since the prevailing Orthodox mode of worship does not require new material. This picture may change in the future but for the time being the only outlet for Israeli composers is offered by the American synagogue.

Several commissioning projects have been carried out so far. The commission under consideration here was given by Rabbi Edward T. Sandrow of Temple Beth-El, Cedarhurst, New York, and assigned to five composers under the editorship of Issachar Miron.

Anyone expecting a fresh breeze from Israel that would stir up the music of the Synagogue will be sadly disappointed. The renaissance of Jewish music which during the last decades has produced a sizable body of progressive works by American Jewish composers seems to have gone unnoticed in Israel if we are to judge by *Kol Rinah b'Ohaley Israel*.

Issachar Miron is represented by six pieces. The stiff organ prelude will hardly be acceptable to discriminating organists. *Tov l'hodot, Shema-Veahavta, Hashkivenu, Veshameru* and *Yigdal* suffer from a tedious application of even numbered measures and a mixture of pseudo-Oriental and European elements. The harmonic style rests on chromatically altered chords of long, long ago; the form of the larger pieces is produced by endless repetition and transposition of small sections, especially glaring in *Yigdal* whose eleven pages of music consist of no more than two sections of eight measures each, alternating all the time (whereby the first section appears once

139

transposed a fourth up), and ending with a short coda. Miron has some attractive melodic material but also a sure hand to stifle it under unsympathetic accompaniments.

Nisan Cohen Melamed contributed *L'chu n'ranenah* and *L'cha Dodi.* This is conventional music in an unflattering sense, a faded imitation of the 19th century manner. *L'cha Dodi,* a piece of unmerciful length annoys with the fixed smile of a bygone charm.

The worst pieces are by Emanuel Amiran who wrote *Adonay Malach, Barchu, Ahavat Olam* and *Y'varechecha.* Amiron is an inept composer who causes embarrassment by ineffective handling of choir and organ and meaningless motion in the organ part, supposed to fill out long notes. It must be said that *Ahavat Olam* starts with a fine melodic turn (I would have wished for a little breathing space before the first three measures are repeated) but the piece is badly harmonized and put together so crudely that every stitch shows.

Benyamin Bar-Am's *Yiyuh l'ratson* and *May the Words* with its ten pages of music is much too long for the place it should occupy in the Service. However, the skillful hand of an experienced composer shows in this piece as well as in his *Vay-chulu.* There is an earnest striving for expression, somewhat thwarted by a harmonic style that still needs clarification. The frequent use of chords in six-four position strikes me as a disturbing mannerism.

Menachem Avidom's *Mi chamochah* opens with two excellent pages which represent the best music of the whole set. Unfortunately, the piece deteriorates steadily after the first two pages. It is surprising that Avidom consistently notates in 6/4 time what obviously is meant to be taken as 3/2. There is also a peculiar handling of the *V'ne-emar ki fada* section. Avidom continues without break in the same manner as in the preceding *Mi chamochah,* thus disregarding the dividing function of the word *V'ne-emar.*

Summing up: *Kol Rinah b'Ohaley Israel* is for the most part an uncreative, in some cases philistine, attempt at Synagogue music, hardly destined to add luster to the reputation of Israeli music. One could surely have expected a more idiomatic musical treatment of a language which, I assume, is the daily speech of these composers.

If men such as Ben Haim, Seter, Lakner—to name only three of Israel's fine composers—had been asked to capture the "Voice of Song in the Tents of Israel," this report might have sounded quite different.

MUSIC OF GERSHON EPHROS

(Tikva Records LPT-87)

We are grateful to Tikva Records for giving us a good sampling of Gershon Ephros' original music. This scholarly cantor, student and friend of Idelsohn's, has won wide acclaim as compiler and editor of the indispensable "Cantorial Anthology." But he is also a versatile composer, quite at ease in the concert hall. True, his concert music confesses freely to its Jewish origin but its secularity is real, and gracefully so.

The Second String Quartet (Aeolian) abounds in Jewish motifs treated in a clean, polyphonic manner; at times, perhaps, a bit overwritten in its diverse layers of independent voices.

The "Children's Suite" (poems by Ch. N. Bialik) for contralto and piano is a work of greatly refined charm, a Jewish counterpart to the Russian example of Moussorgski's Nursery Songs.

Carefully shaped modal melodies betray a sensitive ear for characteristic inflection; the piano part is inventive and at times inobtrusively contrapuntal in canonic play with the voice.

The songs are short but when sixteen small pieces are strung together they make a necklace. I am deliberately choosing this term because in listening to the cycle I could not help thinking of finely wrought Oriental jewelry.

My special affection belongs to certain traits of some individual songs within the cycle: The frightened rabbit singing to the tune of a hunting horn in *Arnevet;* the quiet lyricism of *Keshet* (A Rainbow); the fresh harmonic solution of a Phrygian cadence in *Sus V'Agala* (Horse and Buggy); the humorous re-

143

alism of *Tarngol* (A Cock); the exquisite piano part in *Shovech* (A Dove Cot); the rough diatonic ostinato writing in *S'Charcheret* (Merry-Go-Round).

When performed as a cylce, the sixteen numbers might effectively be cut to about twelve, in order to avoid a sameness of mood in one or another of the pieces.

The two "fillers" on the record, "Vocalise" for soprano, and "Halleluyah" for tenor, are of minor importance as compared to the quartet and the song cycle.

The performances by the Silvermine String Quartet, Antonia Lavanne, soprano, Ruth Brall, contralto, Jacob Marcus, tenor, Bruno Eisner and Reuven Kosakoff, pianists, range from good to fair.

THE SACRED COVENANT AND SING UNTO THE LORD

by Heinrich Schalit

PRAISED BE THE LORD BY DAY by Samuel Adler

For mixed chorus with organ accompaniment
Transcontinental Music Publications

It is pleasant to record the appearance of three fine anthems. Heinrich Schalit, certainly one of the most significant composers of Synagogue music, excels here, as elsewhere, in the purity of a distinctly personal style. He is reaping the fruits of maturity and we are blessed in receiving such gifts.

"The Sacred Covenant" is a full-length anthem written for the dedication of the new sanctury of Temple B'rith Kodesh in Rochester, New York. The words from Exodus ("If you will indeed hearken unto My voice and observe My covenant, then ye shall be unto Me a kingdom of priests and a holy people") are cast in a simple A-B-A-B-Coda form, whereby A is treated as a fugato, B in homophonic style. The second appearance of A is shortened (only three instead of four entrances) and slightly varied. I could have imagined the variation in a more elaborate, more disguised manner but this does not detract from the noble effect of the work as a whole.

Schalit's "Sing unto the Lord" is part of a series of short anthems by different composers commissioned by Temple Emanu-El, Dallas, Texas.

Concise and to the point, the piece is fully effective in conveying a festive mood. Since the organ part doubles the voices throughout I would have welcomed a short organ interlude at the bottom of page 4 before the return to the opening theme.

Samuel Adler's "Praised be the Lord by Day" is an ingratiating number, animated in spirit, solid in workmanship. The *a capella* middle part is especially noteworthy as a sensitive interpretation of the text. A wholesome diatonicism prevails throughout the piece which manages to sound contemporary without recourse to the fashionable chromaticism of our day. Diatonic dissonances have a strength which, I think, goes well with sacred texts.

ADONOY MOH ODOM; SHOLOM ROV; EYL MOLEH RACHAMIM
by Hugo Chaim Adler

A WOMAN OF VALOR; WELCOMING THE SABBATH
by Samuel Adler

Transcontinental Music Publications

The year 1965 marks the tenth *YAHRZEIT* of Hugo Chaim Adler, the well-known cantor-composer who, at the time of his death, left a considerable number of unpublished manuscripts. We are indebted to Transcontinental Music Publications for having chosen this particular year as an occasion to issue some of this material.

Adonoy Moh Odom and *Sholom Rov* are solo songs for baritone or contralto, with organ accompaniment; both very much in the traditional vein, *Sholom Rov* excelling by subtle harmonic turns.

Eyl Moleh Rachamim for tenor cantor (there are optional notes for lower voice), choir and organ is one of Hugo Chaim Adler's strongest compositions and should soon find a place in the repertoire of our Synagogues. The best features of the composer's style appear in a pure and simple presentation: adherence to traditional *chazzanut*, a satisfying change between linear-motivic and chordal accompaniment, grateful writing for the voices. The harmony is unpretentious, yet expressive

147

and of special poignancy in the phrase *adonoy hu nachalosom*. (The textual error on top of page 6 should be corrected: *nishmosom*, instead of *nishmoso*, since the plural version is used throughout).

It is from this piece that a direct line leads from father to son. Samuel Adler's song "A Woman of Valor," though unmistakably the work of a musician of the younger generation, still has its roots in the soil cultivated by the composer's father.

A chassidic tune *(Eshet Chayil)* used with discretion is strengthened by a contrapuntal accompaniment that has its own life but does not overwhelm the singer with distracting motion. There is an inconspicuous canon, a relaxed roaming through several tonalities, a hinted reprise of the beginning—all of them means to take the sting of folksiness out of the composition and to lift it into the sphere of an art song.

The same composer's extended organ prelude "Welcoming the Sabbath," belonging to a series of organ pieces by different composers commissioned by Temple Emanu-El, New York, is a searching, more complicated work. New territory is being explored in strictly linear, mostly three-part, writing. The form is of special interest: A recitative-like opening leads to what seems to become a passacaglia. After two statements of the theme in the pedal it turns out that this is something like a phantasy—passacaglia, with only two more complete appearances of the theme in widely separated places.

INTRODUCTORY REMARKS AT CONCERTS OF THE NEW ENGLAND JEWISH MUSIC FORUM

May 6, 1968—Paul Ben-Haim

In the fiurst century A.D., a Jew from Tarsus, named Saul, saw a vision while traveling to Damascus. He changed his name to Paul, became a missionary for a new faith, and a founder of the Christian Church.

Almost 2000 years later, in 1933, a Jew from Munich, whose name already was Paul, left his native Germany and came to Tel-Aviv. This Paul was a composer who, after his arrival in Palestine, saw a vision of Jewish music which would hardly have appeared to him in another place. He also changed his name and Paul Frankenburger turned into Paul Ben-Haim. Under this name he was destined to become Israel's foremost and best-known composer.

I did not meet Paul Frankenburger in the 1920s while I was a student at the Bavarian State Academy of Music in Munich, the very same school where he, several years earlier, had completed his musical education. But I visited him in 1960 in Tel-Aviv where he received me graciously. In 1966, both he and I taught composition at the Creative Arts Institute of the Union of American Hebrew Congregations. Recently, I conducted the Boston premiere performance of his Sacred Service *Kabbalat Shabbat,* and it was this occasion which brought him to Boston. Tonight we have him as an honored guest at the Jewish Music Forum.

January 24, 1973—Felix Mendelssohn

Felix Mendelssohn was opposed to discussing music, holding the opinion that music speaks its own, non-translatable language. My topic, then, is not so much Mendelssohn's music as the evasive theme of Jewish traces in his personality.

He was the grandson of the Jewish philosopher Moses Mendelssohn who not only influenced the Jewish Emancipation in Germany but was one of the most widely read authors in Europe. His son Abraham was a successful banker and, aside from his mercantile talents, a man of fine intellectual gifts. After his son Felix became famous, Abraham, with subtle irony, used to say of himself: Once I was the son of my father, now I am the father of my son.

Moses Mendelssohn's idea that Judaism was compatible with the acquisition of a general culture was not enough for Abraham, who convinced himself that Judaism should merge with Christianity. His trust that an uncontested, more universal, religion would bestow blessings on its adherents proved a tragic mistake when racial arguments discredited religious affiliation. We don't know what Abraham thought of the constant, by no means harmless, needling of anti-semitic groups directed against newly baptized Jews. But we know today that the needle of the 19th century turned into a sword in 1933.

Abraham's conversion can only be understood as a result of political and social conditions which, at the dawn of liberalism, conspired to make the son of Moses Mendelssohn turn to Christianity.

Let it be said, however, that only a fraction of German Jewry subscribed to Abraham Mendelssohn's ideas. Judaism as a religion and a way of life continued to flourish in Germany, Orthodoxy co-existing with the aspirations of Reform Judaism which introduced changes but did not discard its Jewish identity. Suffice it to mention the names of some distinguished German Jews, contemporary with Abraham and Felix Mendelssohn: Samson Raphael Hirsch, Leopold Zunz, Abraham Geiger, Gabriel Riesser.

Felix Mendelssohn was reared in the Protestant faith, but early in life had some nasty experiences as a "Jewboy." Even his teacher, Karl Friedrich Zelter, a respected musician in his time, introducing the twelve-year old Felix to Goethe as a boy of remarkable talent, could not forego a biting commentary in pidgin Yiddish: It would be "eppes rores"—something rare— he wrote to Goethe, if a Jew grew up to become an artist. As it turned out, Goethe was enchanted with Felix's talent and charm, and followed his career with unfailing interest.

As a mature man, Felix was not always at ease with his Christianity. When his father demanded that he give up the Jewish name Mendelssohn in favor of Bartholdy, Felix demurred. Although he was a loving son who greatly respected his father's judgment, he insisted on keeping his original name. As a compromise, he used Bartholdy in conjunction with Mendelssohn.

His concern with Jewish affairs showed in his jubilant report on the progress of the Jewish Emancipation in England. More than that, he could rise to intemperate anger when his younger sister Rebekka in a letter to him made a condescending remark about an Orthodox Jew. Felix's answer was strong and clear: "What do you mean by saying that you are not hostile to Jews? I hope this was just a joke; otherwise I would take you to task most seriously. It is really sweet of you not to despise your entire family. I expect a full explanation in your next letter."

In spite of these evidences of Mendelssohn's ties to his Jewish origin, I think it quite feasible that Felix, had he not been baptized as a child, might have sought baptism at his own behest. Heinrich Heine put it succinctly, and with a dash of sarcasm, when he called the baptismal certificate an admission ticket to European culture. In Felix Mendelssohn's time, the Jewish Emancipation in Germany had begun but was by no means complete. It was twenty years after Felix's death, in the year 1867, when the last restrictions were lifted. Thus, a man of Felix's genius would have been barred, as a Jew, from fulfilling his musical destiny. What the world could have offered him, without that admission ticket, would have been *Standing room only.*

Looking for Jewish features in Mendelssohn's face is no problem. They are there, unmistakably and abundant. What is Jewish in his music cannot be found by putting a finger on this or that detail. It is rather the work as a whole which pro-

ves the Jew's adaptability to his environment. This ability to
adapt, to absorb, was not acquired overnight. We know it as
the fiuit of a long and grievous history beginning with the
year 70 A.D. when, after the destruction of the Second Temple by the Romans, the Jews were scattered among the nations.

In their best examples, the Jewish contributions to the
culture of other nations were not merely pale imitations. They
rank with the best we know. German Romanticism has nothing lovelier to offer than Mendelssohn's *"Auf Flügeln des
Gesanges"*—On Wings of Song. There we have, within a few
pages, the essence of Romanticism—and that goes not only for
the music but also for the poem, with its dream of love on a
mythical shore in India. Heine's exotic rhyme, pairing
"Gesanges" with *"Ganges"* is the key to that utopian escape from
reality.

Wishing to strengthen my point of the Jew's ability to
create works fully characteristic of his environment, I will give
a few further examples: What could be more Italian than
Salomone Rossi's Madrigals, more French than Offenbach's
"Les Contes d'Hoffmann," what more American than Copland's
"Appalachian Spring" or, in a lighter vein, Broadway's "September Song" by the German Jew Kurt Weill?

One last remark about Mendelssohn: There are still
people who cannot forgive the fact that he came from a wealthy family and never knew hunger and want. According to
their lights, an artist must starve unrecognized in an attic to
gain profundity. This, a thoroughly philistine idea, is amply
contradicted by the life of Goethe, to name only one of the
world's great poets and thinkers.

One cannot deny that Mendelssohn wrote much slick and
facile music but it is not hard either to find in his large output
works that conform to the common idea of depth. I am thinking of the *"Variations Serieuses"* for piano, the String Quartet in
f minor, portions of "Elijah" and so on.

However, I do not believe that depth and sadness have to
be inseparable companions. For me, it is no paradox to call
Mendelssohn's music to Shakespeare's "Midsummer's Night
Dream" profound. It is the other side of profundity, not seen
"through a glass darkly" but reflected in the mirror of a

superior mind capable of turning heavy matter into a weight-
less web.

It may be surprising to some that Brahms, the serious,
bearded Brahms, once said he would give all his works for
Mendelssohn's Hebrides Overture, known as "The Fingals
Cave." Brahms' generosity is both puzzling and admirable,
even if we don't take it at face value. Nevertheless, there is a
core of truth in his statement, and we would do well to pon-
der it.

January 24, 1973—Felix Wolfes (1892-1971)

It is for me a "Duty of the Heart" to say a few words
about Felix Wolfes who died in 1971 and whose memory we
honor with a group of his songs.

Felix Wolfes was a well-known opera conductor in Germany and an outstanding accompanist at the piano. As a
composer he did not have the scope of Mendelssohn, but was
a specialist in writing nothing but songs—all of them in German although he knew French and English well enough.

He left a legacy of more than 200 songs, of which some
forty were published during his lifetime. His search for German poetry that would lend itself to his musical idiom was
constant and, knowing my reading habits, he often wanted me
to suggest new texts to him.

When he once asked me how I went about finding words
for my compositions, I said: "Felix, my case is different. Not
counting some exceptions, I have a steady and, as it happens,
very famous librettist."

"Heavens, who is he?"

My answer was short and surprising:

"King David."

This dialogue may be typical for Felix as well as for me. Felix
never left Judaism but religion—Jewish or otherwise—was not
one of his interests.

What I said about Jewish adaptability in my talk about
Mendelssohn also applies to Felix Wolfes who continued with
refined artistry the style of Hugo Wolf, Richard Strauss and
Hans Pfitzner. In Felix's songs, the singing line is declamatory
rather than self-contained, one strand in a complicated fabric.

He was deeply involved with his texts, his music is poetical and evocative but at the same time tightly constructed with motivic particles pervading a whole song.

As can be expected from a pianist of his stature, his accompaniments are richly elaborated, and it was a great experience to hear him play his own music or the works of other composers. He could conjure up a whole orchestra with an infinite variety of shadings suggesting subtle changes of instrumentation.

As a person, he was delightful: warm-hearted, witty, original, and beloved by all who knew him. The Jewish Music Forum is proud to remember him with what was the essence of his life: the songs he wrote with such mastery and devotion.

EPILOGUE

THE PARABLE OF THE SHOES
(Conclusion of a speech given on October 25, 1972, at the
occasion of my retirement as music director and organist
of Temple Israel, Boston)

. . . . And now, how shall I close? I think I'd like to talk about
my organ shoes. For those of you who may not know it, let me
explain that an organist wears special shoes for playing the
pedals. Such shoes must be light and thin-soled so that the organist can feel the contact with the wooden keys. The older
the shoes get, the better they become, and all organists nurse
their shoes as long as they possibly can. After a number of
years the shoes go the way of all leather and deteriorate into a
disreputable appearance. But as long as they do not fall apart,
the organist will not discard them. To him, the breaks, wrink-
les and creases look like venerable signs of age acquired after
years of wandering through miles and miles of music.

My organ shoes could hardly be shown in a shoe store but
they are by no means ready to go to the garbage can. I think
they still have a few miles in them, and—*im yirtseh Hashem*—if
God wills it, may that also be said about their owner, the man,
musician and composer Herbert Fromm.

APPENDIX

MENDELSSOHN—TWO LETTERS

(translated by the author)

The last part of this hitherto unpublished letter by Felix Mendelssohn refers to his appointment, in 1840 by King Friedrich Wilhelm the Fourth of Prussia, as composer for theater and church, conductor and adviser for the founding of a music school.

Between 1840 and 1843 Mendelssohn commuted between his home in Leipzig, where he was still conductor of the Gewandhaus Orchestra, and Berlin. This double role became so difficult that Mendelssohn, in spite of grave misgivings, decided to move with his family to Berlin, where he had spent his youth. Conditions there were not agreeable and Mendelssohn returned to Leipzig in 1844, still committed, although on a smaller scale, to appear in Berlin for special occasions.

The recipient of this letter is not known, since the envelope is missing. It might well be Professor Joseph Fischhof to whom Mendelssohn's wife Cécile wrote four years later, one day after her husband's death—but we cannot be sure. Felix's letter is important for its own sake, not for the name of the recipient. It shows and confirms the composer's warmth and affability, qualities mirrored in the gentle flourishes of the script.

Dear Professor,

First, my heartiest congratulations on the glad event of your engagement! May Heaven give you its best blessing, happy days, health and everything good I can think of. May you, after many years, look back at the time of your engagement and marriage with the same gratitude and joy as I do on mine—there is nothing better I could wish for you.

But you didn't give me the name of your fiancée, is that the right thing to do? Of course, you said "a very lovely girl" but that is just a title and now I'd like to know her name, the time you have set for your marriage and other details. I hope there will be an opportunity soon to keep me up to date. You know how sincerely I take part in everything concerning you, and most especially in an event which determines so inseparably your future happiness!

And, telling me of this event, you still found time to seek out such a beautiful souvenir for me, to make me such a special gift. This is almost too friendly, too kind. All by themselves, the wonderful workmanship of bottle and glass would have given me the greatest joy but that you sent me that gift in the days of your engagement, giving me two joys at once, and remembering me at a time when everything merges into one thought and all else appears alien and disturbing—for that I cannot thank you enough. I cannot put these beautiful things into the cupboard, as one should for safe keeping, but they must remain standing in the room where I can see them all the time, remembering with gratitude your friendship and kindness!

Your brother will have told you that I spoke to him for a moment at the railroad station as I was about to travel to Berlin. At that time there was such confusion in me and around me that he must have had a bad impression of me, I didn't quite know what I was saying or doing that morning. Please, apologize to him on my behalf, and also forgive the tardiness of this letter. It was only a day before yesterday that I returned from that trip to Berlin. During my stay there my time was taken up with rehearsals, performances and obligations of all kinds, so that I didn't have a free moment.

If things go like this all winter, the prospect looks bad for new compositions I'd like to write. In about four weeks I must move to Berlin with my whole family. I myself am really curious how and if we can live in the atmosphere there.

And now, once more, accept my thanks and my wife's

most cordial congratulations, and remember me in friendship
as your always devoted

Felix Mendelssohn Bartholdy

Leipzig, October 22, 1843

The recipient of Cécile's letter is Joseph Fischhof (1804-
1857) who, in 1833, was appointed professor for piano at the
Vienna Conservatory of Music. He wrote piano music and was
a collector of rare musical manuscripts, among them an au-
tograph of Bach's *Wohltemperiertes Klavier*.

Vesque von Püttlingen, vice president of the Vienna
Gesellschaft der Musikfreunde (Society of Friends of Music) was a
professional musician, student of the famous teacher Simon
Sechter, and composer of several operas. He approached
Mendelssohn in 1839 to conduct his oratorio *Paulus* in Vienna. Mendelssohn accepted, but through misunderstandings
and indiscretions on the part of the Viennese press, he can-
celled the engagement.

What occasioned a renewed correspondence with Vesque
von Püttlingen cannot be gathered from Cécile's letter. She
dated the letter correctly as November 5, but did not give the
year. It was 1847.

Dear Sir:

There cannot be an answer to your last letter to my husband. As I already wrote to Mr. Vesque von Püttlingen, my
husband had a relapse. This was followed by a second, stroke-
like, seizure to which he succumbed last evening. God called
him back on the 4th of November, around half past nine.

His last hours were without pain and he quietly slept
away. Please, tell this to Mr. von Püttlingen as an answer to his
letter which just arrived.

I commend myself as yours,

Cécile Mendelssohn Bartholdy

November 5

The originals of these letters were acquired in Germany by Mr. Heinrich Lieberg, probably within the first decade of this century. They are now in the possession of his daughter-in-law, Mrs. Hilde Lieberg, Newton, Massachusetts, who graciously permitted the use of the material for publication.

MAHLER: DAS LIED VON DER ERDE

A Literary Quarrel

In the last movement of *Das Lied von der Erde* Mahler combines two separate poems from Hans Bethge's German rendition of Chinese poetry, collected under the title *"Die Chinesische Flöte."* I have before me the edition of 1923 which appeared twelve years after Mahler's death. The composer took the poems from an earlier edition which I am unable to locate, and which, perhaps, was different in some details. Those differences, however, if they exist at all, are of no consequence for what I am about to discuss.

The combination of the two poems led to contradictions which make the last movement incomprehensible in a literary sense, and which, surprisingly enough, have never been rectified.

Theodor W. Adorno, in his book *Mahler* (Suhrkamp 1960) devotes pages 190 to 200 to *Das Lied von der Erde.* His approach is analytical in the higher sense of musical philosophy, sometimes (in spite of his denial) psychological, with extended side trips into history and sociology, for which his intellectualized, super-Nietzschean language provides a sharp, if often irritating, tool.

It remains disappointing that he makes no mention at all of the glaring fault which results from the hitching together of the two poems. He fails to put his finger on it, leaving us with no more than "The long last movement, darkly combined of two poems. . ." but he makes not attempt to light a candle.

Adorno, a man of uncommon sensitivity in literary matters, wrote perceptive essays on Goethe, Hölderlin, Eichen-

163

dorff and Heine. Why is he silent in the case of Bethge-Mahler? The main reason must be that he didn't care for the texts, as expressed in these words (page 191):

> *Die kunstgewerblichen Texte Hans Bethge's, denen die*
> *Unsterblichkeit nicht an der Wiege gesungen war. . .*

("The arty texts of Bethge to which immortality was not sung at the cradle. . .")

Another reason could be attributed to the height from which he viewed Mahler. The literary crack—large at close range—seemed so tiny that it didn't merit further investigation.

Similarly, though for different reasons, Bruno Walter, who conducted the first performance of the work after Mahler's death, was not aware of the literary lapse. In his autobiography *(Theme and Variation)* he is only interested in questions concerning a practicing musician. Talking about the premiere performance, he says: "I had chosen a baritone in place of an alto. Mahler himself had been of two minds about this. His instructions permitted the alternative, and so I thought I owed him the experiment. . . but I have never repeated it because I had become convinced that an alto was better able to fulfill the vocal demands made by the part, and that in the six songs the contrast between the sounds of an alto and a tenor voice was more welcome to the ear than that between two male voices."

Before discussing the last movement in greater detail, it might be well to review the whole work from a literary angle in relationship to the musical setting.

In the Table of Contents Mahler is consistent. He wants two different voices in alternation which is stated clearly in the parenthetic assignments after each title. Movements I, III and V are marked "Tenor," II, IV and VI, "Alt oder Bariton." But in the actual score he says only "Altstimme" in IV and VI, without mentioning the possibility of a baritone. No. II is the exception. Bethge's title reads *"Die Einsame im Herbst"* whereas Mahler, considering the chance of a baritone, changed the title to *"Der Einsame im Herbst."*

When the voice begins, after the extended orchestral introduction, Mahler remarks: "Altstimme (kann eventuell auch von einem Bariton übernommen werden)"—"Alto voice (may

possibly be taken by a baritone)". The change of the title from
the feminine to the masculine gender makes accommodation
for a baritone but leaves the alto voice, although apparently
Mahler's first choice, unaccounted for—unless we accept the
alto as a sufficient substitute for a baritone.

In the 18th century opera tradition it was not uncommon
to have a young man sung by a female voice: Cherubino in
Mozart's Figaro, Octavian in Strauss' Rosenkavalier which
happens to play in the 18th century. This practice can hardly
be applied to Mahler's "Lied von der Erde" where just about everything speaks against such a procedure.

The equivocation could have been avoided by calling the
piece "Einsamkeit im Herbst" (Loneliness in Autumn). The
poem, as such, stands in no immediate contradiction to either
a male or a female voice, although the tone, the whole sensibility of the words, is more easily associated with a woman
than with a man.

Following Mahler's plan of alternation, No. IV cannot be
sung by a tenor who already had I and III. In the score, disregarding the Table of Contents, Mahler says only
"Altstimme." Here, a conflict arises between the text and the
choice of a female voice. The subtly erotic overtones of the
poem, distinctly male in nature, make the alto voice unsuited
to the words which describe girls gathering flowers and watch-
ing with agitation young men riding by on horseback. Here is
the second stanza (referring to the girls):

Goldne Sonne webt um die Gestalten,
Spiegelt sie im blanken Wasser wider.
Sonne spiegelt ihre schlanken Glieder,
Ihre süssen Augen wider,
Und der Zephir hebt mit Schmeichelkosen
Das Gewebe ihrer Ärmel auf,
Führt den Zauber ihrer Wohlgerüche
Durch die Luft.

(The golden sun around their forms
Mirrors them in the clear waters.
Sun relfects their slender limbs,
The sweet eyes,
And Zephyr lifts with coaxing flattery
The fabric of their sleeves,

Carrying enchanting odors
Through the air.)

In spite of what has been said so far, my misgivings would
not have been enough to subtitle this essay "A Literary Quarrel," were it not for the last movement, which, as Mahler left
it, is unsupportable from a literary point of view. According to
Mahler's self-imposed law of alternation, the piece cannot be
assigned to the tenor, which again leaves us with alto or
baritone. Mahler definitely decided for "Altstimme" when the
voice begins at ⟨3⟩ , after the introduction. The two poems, sup-
plying the text, have something in common, and are printed
in Bethge's book on facing pages.

In Erwartung des Freundes
(Expecting the Friend)
Der Abschied des Freundes
(The Friend's Farewell)

The connection is explained in Bethge's remarks at the
end of the book:

"Mong-Kao-Jen was closely befriended by the author of
the next poem, Wang-Wei. The friend, expected by
Mong-Kao-Jen, is Wang-Wei. He, in turn, addressed
his poem "The Friend's Farewell" to Mong-Kao-Jen."

Thus, if Bethge's explanation is correct, we have a clear
case of a farewell scene between two men, which would call
for a baritone. However, after the second movement, Mahler
abandoned the option between alto and baritone, by specify-
ing in the score "Altstimme" in IV and VI. Surely, most musicians will agree with me that a composer's wish, as set down
in the actual score, supersedes the somewhat mechanical order
of a Table of Contents. Is the alto voice really supposed to
carry off a scene between two men? I think not. Bethge's
footnote about the two poems is not mentioned by Mahler,
and is unknown to the audience. The listener hears a woman,
and his natural reaction may be summed up in a simple equa-
tion: A woman is meant when a woman is singing.

Mahler, aware of this, made some changes in the first
poem which strengthen the impression that it is a woman expecting her male friend. The last line of the first poem, in my
edition, reads:

O kämst du, kämst du, ungetreuer Freund.
("Why don't you come, unfaithful friend.")
Since the friend appears later, Mahler substituted this line
with a vague, high-flying sentence, probably of his own writ-
ing:
> *O Schönheit, o ewigen Liebens lebenstrunkne Welt.*
("O beauty, o world intoxicated by eternal love.")
The second poem, being a farewell, causes Mahler to make
another change in the first poem.

Bethge: *Ich stehe hier und harre des Freundes*
        Der zu kommen mir versprach
        (I am standing here, waiting for my friend,
        Who promised to come.)

Mahler: *Ich stehe hier und harre meines Freundes,*
        Ich harre sein zum letzten Lebewohl.
        (I am standing here, waiting for my friend,
        Waiting for the last farewell).

      The two poems are separated by a long,
symphonic interlude (the anxious waiting period before the
friend arrives?) but that the two parts are conceived as one
movement is a point Mahler strongly emphasizes by using
conspicuous motifs of the first part also in the second section.
      The second poem, in Bethge's version, begins thus:
> *Ich stieg vom Pferd und reichte ihm*
> *Den Trunk des Abschieds dar.*
> (I descended from the horse and offered him
> The farewell drink.)

The person having sung the first part and continuing into the
second cannot be pictured on horseback, be it man or woman.
As proof, I quote two lines from the first poem:
> *Ich wandle auf und nieder mit meiner Laute*
> *Auf Wegen, die von weichem Grase schwellen.*
> (I am walking up and down with my lute
> On paths abounding with soft grass.)

Hence, Mahler, introducing the other person as a man:
> *Er stieg vom Pferd und reichte ihm*   '
> *Den Trunk des Abschieds dar.*
> (He descended from the horse and
> offered him the farewell drink).

It is this ominous "ihm" (him) which comes as a shock since it destroys the expectation prepared for by the preceding part. Bethge continues:

> *Ich fragte ihn wohin*
> *Und auch warum er reisen wolle.*
>
> (I asked him where,
> And also why he wished to travel.)

Mahler, with heightened intensity:

> *Er fragte ihn wohin er führe*
> *Und auch warum es müsste sein.*
>
> (He asked him where he wished to go
> And also why it had to be.)

(There are significant other changes at the end of the poem, but, having no bearing on the purpose of this essay, they need not be discussed here.)

If ones leaves the words as Mahler used them, the woman, in the second part of the movement, would be cast in the role of a spectator who narrates a farewell scene between two men. This makes no sense, and stands, by implication, against Mahler's changes in the first poem which anticipates a woman-man situation. In order to preserve this concept, it is perfectly valid to have the woman continue in the second part of the movement, telling what her friend said. The friend does not necessarily have to speak himself. (The tenor who was employed in the first, third and fifth movements cannot be brought in here for the comparatively short part, the tessitura being too low.)

Keeping in mind that we hear the same voice as before, we must ask ourselves: Why the sudden shift from the involved "I" to the diminished participation of "THEY"? Without warning, the gears are thrown into reverse, with the inevitable jolt resulting from such action. The music itself, after the initial recitative, has the passionate impact of direct speech and cannot be interpreted as a report, no matter how sympathetic the reporter may be.

To preserve the continuity, two minor changes in the wording have to be made which would not entail any change in the music.

Page 87, vocal score:

> *Er stieg vom Pferd und reichte mir*

Den Trunk des Abschieds dar.
Ich fragte ihn, etc.
(He descended from the horse and
offered me The farewell drink. I asked him,
etc.)
Page 89, vocal score:
"Du mein Freund" would have to be changed to
"Du meine Freundin."
    A point could be made by recalling that the alto voice, as
in No. II, might stand for a baritone, and that Mahler actually
conceived the last movement, in its second part, as a scene between two men. It is a difficult situation which, nevertheless,
could be thought of as an intended abstraction, although such
thinking-round-the-corner would be hard to accept. And even
so, the first of the suggested changes would be necessary to
insure a continuity between the two sections.
    Finally, what of the idea that Mahler didn't want a con-
tinuity, that he looked on the second poem as independent of
the first? Such an argument, aside from what has been said in
the previous pages, falls with the unity of the music which
demands textual unity as well.
    Mahler's vacillation—alto or baritone—created difficulties
in II and IV which might be overlooked, but endangered the
last movement to a point where repair becomes unavoidable.
Having observed that Mahler had no hesitation to bend words
to his purpose, we are certainly justified in making small
changes if they serve to clarify the precarious junction of two
poems.
    The half-hearted remark in II ("may possibly be taken by
a baritone") and the lack of a choice in IV and VI make me
believe that Mahler had an alto in mind for II, IV and VI.
Bethge's explanation that the two poems of No. VI belong together as a farewell between two men seems to be the only reason for giving an option in the Table of Contents, if not in
the music itself.
    The fact that most audiences don't read texts close
enough to be aware of an untenable literary situation, must
not deter us from straightening out what Mahler, for unknown reasons, left undone.

INDEX